Commercial Travellers' Association of Canada

Act of Incorporation of the Commercial Travellers'

Association of Canada and Amendments

Commercial Travellers' Association of Canada

Act of Incorporation of the Commercial Travellers' Association of Canada and Amendments

ISBN/EAN: 9783337209032

Printed in Europe, USA, Canada, Australia, Japan

Cover: Foto ©ninafisch / pixelio.de

More available books at **www.hansebooks.com**

Commercial Travellers' Association

OF CANADA

Toronto, October 28th, 1919.

Dear Sir:—

In pursuance of By-law 91, I beg to inform you that I have received notice that the following change in By-laws Nos. 67 & 68 is to be proposed at the Annual Meeting to be held on Saturday, the 27th day of December next, that is to say: Present By-law No. 67—Clause (cc) and Clause (cccc):

By-law 67—Clause (cc)

Provided that the "Mortuary Benefit" shall, so far as possible, be maintained at a maximum of $1,000, the Directors may in each year declare that the "Mortuary Benefit" for the ensuing year shall be $1,000.

And in order to provide funds to pay said maximum "Mortuary Benefit" of $1,000, in the event of the allotment and surplus allotment being exceeded, the Directors shall, by resolution, declare that each member who shall have been admitted and who shall renew his membership for the then ensuing year, shall, in addition to his annual subscription, pay to the Association an additional contribution of such sum as may be determined by the Directors, having regard to the funds of the Association available for the payment of the said "Mortuary Benefit."

' (cccc) If any member liable for such further contribution shall fail to pay the amount thereof on or before the first day of April following the publication of the Directors' report containing such resolution, the "Mortuary Benefit" payable in respect of his membership shall thenceforth be reduced by twenty-five per cent., and his beneficiaries, or legal representatives, shall upon his death be entitled to receive only seventy-five per cent. of his share in said maximum "Mortuary Benefit" of $1,000, which said share shall be ascertained in the manner provided in this By-law; but any member making default, as aforesaid, shall not thereafter be called upon by any resolution of the Directors nor shall he be liable to pay any further contribution under this By-law beyond the amount of his annual subscription.

Proposed Amendments.

Proposed to repeal the first paragraph of Clause (cc) of By-law 67.

To remove from second paragraph of Clause (cc) of By-law 67 in second line "of $1,000."

To remove "$1,000" in Clause (cccc) in eleventh line.

By-law 68—Clause (aaa)

Provided also that as to any persons admitted to membership on and after the first day of January, 1906, under By-law 14, the whole of the maximum "Mortuary Benefit" shall be payable only in case such member shall have paid his subscriptions and shall have been a member for fifteen or more consecutive years immediately preceding his decease; and for this purpose the year in which the death occurs shall be counted as one year, and such benefit shall be reduced one-fifteenth for each year of consecutive membership less than fifteen.

By-law 68—Clause (aaaa)

Provided also, that the amount of such benefit as to persons admitted to membership on and after the first day of January, 1906, under By-law 14, shall be regulated as to scale according to the age of the applicant at his birthday next following the date of his admission, and shall be payable upon the table following, viz.:

Age at birthday next following admission.	Proportion of benefi payable.
25 years and under.......	The whole benefit.
26 to 30 years inclusive...	85 p.c. of whole benefit.
31 to 35 " " ...	75 " "
36 to 40 " " ...	60 " "
41 to 45 " " ...	50 " "
46 to 50 " " ...	35 " "
51 to 55 " " ...	25 " "
56 to 60 and over ...	15 " "

Subject always to a proportional reduction of one-fifteenth for each year required to complete the full term of fifteen consecutive years, as required by Section (aaa) of this By-law.

Proposed Amendments to By-law 68.

In By-law 68, Clause (aaa), where the word "fifteen" occurs, substitute the word "ten," and where the word "one-fifteenth" occurs substitute the word "one-tenth" and "less than fifteen" to read "less than ten."

In Clause (aaaa), By-law 68, where the words "one-fifteenth" occur, substitute "one-tenth"; instead of the words "full term of fifteen consecutive years," substitute "ten consecutive years."

(A)

Commercial Travellers' Association

OF CANADA

+++++++ +++++

Additional Accident Insurance

+++++ ++ ++ ++

$5,000

In case of Death from Accident.

$25.00

Per Week Indemnity in case of Accident.

$12.00

Total Yearly Cost, or

3½c.

Per Day, payable in

4

Quarterly Payments.

___

SAFE, PROMPT, LIBERAL.

+++++++++ ++

MAXIMUM BENEFITS.

___

$5,000 in the event of Death resulting from Accident.

$5,000 in the event of Loss of Limbs resulting from Accident.

$5,000 in the event of Permanent Loss of Sight of Both Eyes resulting from Accident.

$1,666.66 in the event of Loss of Limb resulting from Accident.

$25 per week for 26 weeks in the event of Total Disabling Injury resulting from Accident.

Special Benefits in our Policy.

NONE LIKE THEM.

All claims for Injury paid within 2 months.

If Death occurs from Accident within 6 months, payment made of $5,000.

All Maximum Benefits paid if resulting within 6 months.

No deduction from Weekly Indemnity of $25 because your salary or income is less than $25 per week.

Payment made for all Accidents during the year, notwithstanding one extends to 26 weeks.

NOTE THE ABOVE POINTS.

++ +++ +++ +++ +++ +++

Facts re Additional Accident

Insurance.

Members can pay the full yearly cost in one payment if they wish. Total, $12.

Remember your Policy will cover $5,000 in the event of loss of limbs resulting from accident; $5,000 in the event of permanent loss of sight of both eyes resulting from accident; $1,666.66 in the event of loss of limb resulting from accident; $25 per week for 26 weeks in the event of total disabling injury resulting from accident.

No company in Canada ever offered commercial travellers $5,000 accident insurance for $12 until your Board of Directors made the arrangement for you.

The profits of this Branch will go to your own Association, then why spend your money on outsiders. If you obtain a policy through an outside agent, although at the same rate, the agent and company is the gainer and the Association the *loser*, therefore send your application direct to the Association.

Please bear in mind that you would have paid one-half more for your accident insurance had it not been for your Board of Directors making the above arrangements. Speak at once your appreciation of their efforts, your confidence in the Association, by sending in your application.

CAN ANY ONE AFFORD

To be without Accident Insurance?

Clearly, NO.

~~~~~~~~~~

Examine the Following Table.

Analysis of Claim List covering 15 years experience of one of the largest Accident Companies in the world.	1879 to 1893
RIDING, DRIVING AND WALKING, OUT-DOOR accidents on the road or in the streets, through frost, storms. lightning, orange peel, reckless driving by others, etc	8,334
BUSINESS AND PROFESSIONAL ACCIDENTS, all classes of working and manufacturing risks, surgical cases, etc...	4,738
HOUSE AND DOMESTIC CASUALTIES, ARISING from moving up and down stairs, or about the rooms, in the yard, and in the garden, through gas explosions, fire, etc....	2,731
TRAVELLING by river, sea, railway, tramway, and other conveyances, on business and on pleasure..	665
INJURIES caused by animals, birds and insects....	363
ACCIDENTS ARISING out of sports and pastimes, at cricket, football, boating, bicycling, bathing, fishing, hunting or skating..................	1,977
	18,808

It will be seen that out of 18,808 claims, 11,428 injuries [1st, 3rd and 5th items, over 60 per cent.] were received entirely independent of the occupation of the insured, while only 4,738, or about 25 per cent., resulted from the special hazard of the business engaged in.

A large percentage of injuries are caused by cuts, bruises, reckless driving by others, hanging signs, street cars, herdics, runaway horses, elevators, explosions of steam or gas, electric light wires in and out of position, and numberless other hazards to which every one is exposed.

Don't take any risks, send for Application in Commercial Travellers' Additional Accident and get a Policy without any delay. Only $3.00 per quarter, or $12.00 per year.

ASSESSMENT SYSTEM

The Commercial Travellers'
Mutual Benefit Society,
TORONTO.

++++++++ ++

One of the **Four Assessment** Companies Licensed by the Dominion Government.

++++++++++

Six Assessments Each Year.

Cheap and Absolutely Safe.

++++++++++

Travellers have the option of taking $1,000 or $2,000 insurance.

++++++++++

Send your name and address for Application Form to

W. G. H. LOWE, Secretary,
51 Yonge Street,
TORONTO, ONT.

ACT OF INCORPORATION

OF THE

Commercial Travellers'

ASSOCIATION

OF CANADA

AND AMENDMENTS.

ALSO

BY-LAWS

As Revised by the Annual Meeting, Dec. 29, 1887. Annual
Reports, 1888-1893, and other information.

HEAD OFFICE, 51 YONGE STREET, TORONTO.

1894.

Toronto :

PRINTED BY HUNTER, ROSE & CO.

SPECIAL NOTICES.

In every case of claim arising from ACCIDENT, it is imperative to notify the Secretary of all particulars, as soon after the occurrence as possible, so that the same may be investigated without delay.

Members are not permitted, under any circumstances whatever, to lend their Certificates, and must in all cases show them when required, to *any* officer of any Railway r Steamboat Company from whom privileges are obtained. A refusal to do so renders members liable to severe penalty.

It is desired by the Transportation Companies and urged by the Directors of the Association, that members having baggage to check will see that their trunks are at the depot at least *fifteen minutes* before advertised time of starting.

Members will bear in mind that the regular General Meetings of the Association will be held on the FIRST SATURDAY in March, June, September, and December, at eight o'clock, p.m., ten to form a quorum.

Directors meet on the LAST SATURDAY in every nth, at two o'clock, p.m. None of these meetings will be further advertised.

It is important that members of the Association should see that their correct *addresses* are in the hands of the Secretary, so as to receive promptly any special communication that may be sent out from the Association.

Officers and Directors for 1894.

C. C. VAN NORMAN .... President.
R. H. GRAY .... 1st Vice-President.
JAS. HAYWOOD ...... 2nd Vice-President.
J. C. BLACK .... Treasurer.
JAS. SARGANT ...... Secretary.

DIRECTORS.

M. C. ELLIS, | T. P. HAYES, (Died
C. E. KYLE, | JOHN ORR, Mar. 15.)
JOHN BURNS, | E E. STARR,
JOHN MULDREW, | GEO. WEST.
R. H. COSBIE, | H. GOODMAN, (Elec'd
Mar. 31.)

HAMILTON

H. G. WRIGHT ...... 1st Vice-President.
JOHN HOOPER ...... 2nd Vice-President.

DIRECTORS

W. E. LA CHANCE, | FRED. JOHNSON,
J. H. HERRING, | E. A. DALLEY,
W. G. REID. | ROSS R. WILSON.

GUELPH

C. AULD .... Vice-President.
GEORGE HILL ...... Director.

BRANTFORD

J. S. HAMILTON | D. J. WATEROUS.

MONTREAL

S. O. SHOREY ...... Vice-President.
C. McARTHUR, C. L. SHOREY .. Directors.

KINGSTON

M. S. SUTHERLAND, B. W. ROBERTSON, Directors.

BERLIN

C. NIEHAUS, | M. A. WHITING.

WINNIPEG

G. F. GALT .... Vice-President.
W. L. BROCK, H. MILLER .. Directors.

VICTORIA

A. C. FLUMMERFELT | R. MARTIN.

(3)

Officers and Directors for 1893.

C. C. VAN NORMAN   ..   ..   President.
R. H. GRAY   ..   ..   1st Vice-President.
JAMES HAYWOOD   ..   2nd Vice-President.
J. C. BLACK   ..   ..   Treasurer.
JAMES SARGANT   ..   ..   ..   Secretary.

DIRECTORS

JOS. KILGOUR,	T. P. HAYES,
W. B. DACK,	G. E. HAMILTON,
M. C. ELLIS.	JOHN A. ROSS,
JOHN EVERETT,	JOHN ORR.
C. E. KYLE,	

HAMILTON

H. G. WRIGHT   ..   ..   1st Vice-President.
JOHN HOOPER   ..   ..   ..   2nd Vice-President.

DIRECTORS

W. E. LA CHANCE	FRED. JOHNSON,
J. H. HERRING	E. A. DALLEY,
W. G. REID,	ROSS R. WILSON.

GUELPH

C. AULD   ..   ..   Vice-President
GEORGE HILL   ..   ..   Director.

BRANTFORD

J. S. HAMILTON | D. J. WATEROUS.

MONTREAL

S. O. SHOREY   ..   ..   ..   Vice-President.
C. McARTHUR, C. L. SHOREY ..   ..   Directors.

KINGSTON

M. S. SUTHERLAND, B. W. ROBERTSON, Directors.

BERLIN

C. NIEHAUS, | M. A. WHITING.

WINNIPEG

G. F. GALT   ..   ..   Vice-President.
W. L. BROCK, H. MILLER   ..   ...   Directors.

VICTORIA

A. C. FLUMMERFELT, | R. MARTIN.

Officers and Directors for 1892.

OHN BURNS	.. ..	President.
C. VAN NORMAN	.. ..	1st Vice-President.
R. J. ORR ..	.. .. ..	2nd Vice-President.
R. H. GRAY	.. ..	Treasurer.
AMES SARGANT	.. .. ..	Secretary.

DIRECTORS

OSEPH KILGOUR,	JAMES HAYWOOD,
JOHN EVERETT,	M. C. ELLIS,
H. S. STANBURY,	JOHN ORR,
W. B. DACK,	J. A. ROSS.
H. MORRISON,	

HAMILTON

G. E. HAMILTON ..	.. ..	1st Vice-President.
H. G. WRIGHT	.. .. ..	2nd Vice-President.

DIRECTORS

H. BEDLINGTON,	W. G. REID,
W. E. LA CHANCE,	E. A. DALLEY,
JOHN HOOPER,	J. H. HERRING.

GUELPH

C. AULD ..	.. .. ..	Vice-President.
GEORGE HILL	... .	Director.

BRANTFORD

J. S. HAMILTON, D. J. WATEROUS ..   Directors.

MONTREAL

S. O. SHOREY	.. ..	Vice-President.
C. McARTHUR, C. L. SHOREY ..	..	Directors.

KINGSTON

M. S. SUTHERLAND, B. W. ROBERTSON, Directors.

BERLIN

C. NIEHAUS,   M. A. WHITING.

WINNIPEG

J. B. MATHER,	.. .. ..	Vice-President.
GEO. GALT, H. MILLER	.. ..	Directors.

VICTORIA

J. C. MARSHALL,   R. MARTIN.

Officers and Directors for 1891.

JOHN BURNS .. .. President.
C. C. VAN NORMAN .. .. 1st Vice-President.
R. J. ORR .. .. 2nd Vice-President.
R. H. GRAY.. .. .. Treasurer.
JAMES SARGANT .. .. .. Secretary.

DIRECTORS

JOS. KILGOUR,	JOHN ORR,
H. S. DAVISON,	W. B. DACK.
H. S. STANBURY,	H. MORRISON,
JOHN EVERETT,	M. C. ELLIS.
JAMES HAYWOOD,	

HAMILTON

G. E. HAMILTON, H. G. WRIGHT, Vice-Presidents.

DIRECTORS

JOHN HOOPER,	F. TOBIAS,
J. H. HERRING,	W. E. LA CHANCE,
E. A. DALLEY,	W. G. REID.

GUELPH

C. AULD .. .. Vice-President.
GEO. HILL .. .. Director.

BRANTFORD

J. S. HAMILTON, D. J. WATEROUS .. Directors.

MONTREAL

S. O. SHOREY .. .. .. Vice-President.
C. McARTHUR, C. L. SHOREY .. .. Directors.

KINGSTON

M. S. SUTHERLAND, B. W. ROBERTSON, Directors.

BERLIN

C. NIEHAUS, | M. A. WHITING.

WINNIPEG

J. B. MATHER .. .. .. Vice-President.
GEO. GALT, H. MILLER, ... Directors.

VICTORIA

J. C. MARSHALL, | R. MARTIN.

(6)

Officers and Directors for 1890.

A. A. ALLAN	President.
JOHN BURNS	1st Vice-President.
C. C. VAN NORMAN	2nd Vice-President.
R. H. GRAY...	Treasurer.
JAMES SARGANT	Secretary.

DIRECTORS

JOSEPH KILGOUR,	H. STANBURY,
JAMES HAYWOOD,	T. P. HAYES,
J. H. DEVANEY,	JOHN ORR,
H. S. DAVISON,	JOHN EVERETT.
H. MORRISON,	

HAMILTON
E. A. DALLEY, W. G. REID .. Vice-Presidents.

DIRECTORS

GEO. E. HAMILTON,	J. H. HERRING,
JOHN HOOPER,	H. BEDLINGTON,
H. G. WRIGHT,	R. COLEMAN.

MONTREAL
S. O. SHOREY .. .. .. Vice-President.
C. McARTHUR, C. L. SHOREY ... .. Directors.

KINGSTON
M. S. SUTHERLAND, J. B. ROBERTSON, Directors.

BRANTFORD
J. S. HAMILTON, D. J. WATEROUS .. Directors.

BERLIN
CHAS. NIEHAUS, M A. WHITING .. Directors.

GUELPH
C. AULD .. .. Vice-President.
J. B. ARMSTRONG... .. .. .. Director.

WINNIPEG
J. B. MATHER .. .. .. Vice-President.
GEO. GALT, H. MILLER .. .. Directors.

VICTORIA
J. C. MARSHALL, G. LESORR .. .. Directors.

Officers and Directors for 1889,

A. A. ALLAN .. .. President.
JOHN BURNS .. .. .. 1st Vice-President.
C. C. VAN NORMAN .. .. 2nd Vice-President,
R. H. GRAY.. .. .. Treasurer.
JAMES SARGANT.. .. .. .. Secretary.

DIRECTORS

JOSEPH KILGOUR, | T. P. HAYES,
R. J. ORR. | H. MORRISON,
JOHN ORR, | JOSEPH DEVANEY,
JAMES HAYWOOD, | GEORGE WEST.
H. S. DAVISON, |

HAMILTON

E. A. DALLEY, W. G. REID .. Vice-Presidents.

DIRECTORS

H. G. WRIGHT, | J. H. HERRING,
R. T. STEELE, | J. S. REID,
GEO. E. HAMILTON, | H. BEDLINGTON.

MONTREAL

S. O. SHOREY .. .. .. Vice-President.
C. McARTHUR, C. L. SHOREY .. Directors.

KINGSTON

M. S. SUTHERLAND, B. W. ROBERTSON, Directors

LONDON

M. T. LESTER, P. J. WATT .. ... Directors.

BRANTFORD

J. S. HAMILTON, D. J. WATEROUS .. Directors.

BERLIN

CHAS. NIEHAUS, M. A. WHITING .. Directors.

GUELPH

C. AULD .. .. Vice-President.
J. B. ARMSTRONG.. .. .. .. Director.

WINNIPEG

J. B. MATHER .. .. .. Vice-President.
GEO. GALT, H. MILLER .. .. Directors.

VICTORIA

C. L. CUSACK, J. C. MARSHALL .. Directors.

(8)

CERTIFICATES OF MEMBERSHIP

TORONTO.—At Office of Secretary, James Sargant, Commercial Travellers' Building, 51 Yonge Street, Toronto.

HAMILTON.—W. S. Duffield (W. E. Sanford Manufacturing Co.)

MONTREAL.—S. O. Shorey (H. Shorey & Co.)

GUELPH.—D. Barlow (Guelph Enterprise Co.)

KINGSTON.—M. S. Sutherland (Fenwick, Hendry & Co.)

BRANTFORD.—E W. H. Van Allen (A. Harris, Son, & Co.)

WINNIPEG.—M. H. Miller (M. H. Miller & Co.)

BERLIN.—C. Huehan (L. J. Breithaupt & Co.)

BROCKVILLE—G. A. McMullen (Jas. Hall & Co.)

VICTORIA, B.C.——H. L. Roberts, Erskine Mill Co.

QUEBEC.—L. S. Odell (H. J. Fisk & Co.)

ST. JOHN, N.B.—R. Rogers, 99 Prince William St.

HALIFAX, N.S.—W. D. CAMERON, 111 Granville St.

FORMS OF APPLICATION.

Form One.   Admission.

To the President, Officers and Directors of the Commercial Travellers' Association of Canada:

I,   of   *   , being a Commercial Traveller, travelling at least four months every year, and representing the establishment of   engaged in the business of   at   ·   do hereby make application to become a member of your Association, and do promise, if admitted, to faithfully observe all the Rules and By-laws which may from time to time be in force.

My age next birthday will be   years, and I make   my beneficiary, relationship

Age (if a minor). ·

Toronto,   , 189

Applicant.

Recommended.   *Address.*

Director's.

Firm.

Form Two.   Honorary Membership.

To the President, Officers and Directors of the Commercial Travellers' Association of Canada :

I,   of   having been a Travelling Member of the said Association for five or more consecutive years, do hereby make application to become an Honorary Member of the Association, and promise to observe faithfully all Rules and By-laws which may from time to time be in force.

My age next birthday will be   years, and I make   my beneficiary, relationship

Age (if a minor).

Toronto,   , 189

Applicant.

Address,

Form Three. Renewal Application for 1894.

*To the President, Officers and Directors of the Commercial
Travellers' Association of Canada:*

1. Name in full ....
2. Age next birthday ....No. of Certificate for 1893
   ....For 1894.................
3. P.O. Address, No. and Street ....
4. Firm represented ....
5. Kind of business........................ ....
6. Address..
7. Do you solicit orders from dealers or manufacturers
   only ?.......................................
8. Do you ever solicit orders from consumers ?..........
   ....
9. About how many days in the year do you travel
   soliciting orders ?...........................
10. About how many pounds of baggage do you carry ?
    ....
11. Name of Person in whose favor Accident and Mortuary
    Certificate is made payable.....................
12. Relationship................................
13. Age (if a minor)...........................

I hereby certify that I have carefully read the Application herewith presented, and have answered all the questions herein contained, truthfully and to the best of my knowledge and belief.

Dated at...........this........day of............
A.D. 189..

Signature.......................................

NOTE.—*Signatures* must in all cases be in applicant's own handwriting.

RAILWAY ARRANGEMENTS.

1.—The following railway companies issue station to station tickets to travelling members of this Association at 2¼c. per mile, holders of such tickets are allowed to carry 300 lbs. of baggage free, permitting same to be checked to destination with stop-over privileges. Tickets can be procured at all railway depots, good from Friday noon to return up to Monday evening, but only from starting point to residence named on Certificate ; or Toronto, Montreal, Hamilton and London.

> Canadian Pacific Railway (Eastern Division), including Sault Ste. Marie Branch.
> Canadian P ·ific Railway (Western Division), 3c. per mile to Canmore.
> Central Ontario Railway.
> Central Vermont   "
> Erie and Huron   "
> Grand Trunk   "
> International   "
> Kingston and Pembroke Railway.
> Michigan Central (Canada Division) Railway.
> Niagara Central.
> Montreal and Sorel Railway.
> Nova Scotia Railway.
> Prince Edward Island Railway.
> Quebec Central Railway.
> Quebec and Lake St. John Railway.
> Lake Erie, Essex and Detroit River Railway.
> New Brunswick Railways (operated by C.P.R)
> Canada Eastern Railway.
> Windsor and Annapolis Railway.
> Brantford, Waterloo and Lake Erie Railway
> Great North-West Central Railway.
> Brockville, Westport and Sault Ste. Marie Railway.
> Drummond County Railway.

Ottawa & Gatineau Valley Railway, Prov. of Que.
Salisbury & Harvey Railway, Prov. of N.B.
Shore Line Railway,   "   "
Central Railway,   "   "
Cumberland Railway, Prov. of N.B.
Niagara Falls Park & River Railway (rates to be
    had from Secretary).

II.—The following railway company grants to travelling
members of the Association passenger rates at 2c. per
mile, and allows 300 lbs. of baggage free, which can be
checked to destination with lay-over privileges, namely :

Intercolonial Railway of Canada.

———

Northern Pacific Railway, Manitoba, same rate as
    C.P R.
Canadian Pacific Mountain Division, $3\frac{1}{2}$c. per mile
    with 300 lbs. baggage free.

III.—The Western Counties Railway charge ordinary
passenger rates, allowing to travelling members 300 lbs.
of baggage free, which can be checked to destination with
lay-over privileges.

IV.—For rates to New York, Chicago or European
ports, apply to the Secretary.

COMMERCIAL TRAVELLERS' RAILWAY PASSEN-
GER RATES.

The following are fares to be charged Commercial Travellers, made upon the basis of 2¼ cents per mile. Find the mileage in the first column, and the figures shown opposite in the second column will be the correct fare :—

Miles.	Fare.	Miles.	Fare.	Miles.	Fare.	Miles.	Fare.
	cts.		$ cts.		$ cts.		$ cts.
1	5	36	80	71	1 60	106	2 40
2	5	37	85	72	1 60	107	2 40
3	5	38	85	73	1 65	108	2 45
4	10	39	90	74	1 65	109	2 45
5	10	40	90	75	1 70	110	2 50
6	15	41	95	76	1 70	111	2 50
7	15	42	95	77	1 75	112	2 50
8	20	43	95	78	1 75	113	2 55
9	20	44	1 00	79	1 80	114	2 55
10	25	45	1 00	80	1 80	115	2 60
11	25	46	1 05	81	1 85	116	2 60
12	30	47	1 05	82	1 85	117	2 65
13	30	48	1 10	83	1 90	118	2 65
14	30	49	1 10	84	1 90	119	2 70
15	35	50	1 15	85	1 90	120	2 70
16	35	51	1 15	86	1 95	121	2 75
17	40	52	1 20	87	1 95	122	2 75
18	40	53	1 20	88	2 00	123	2 75
19	45	54	1 20	89	2 00	124	2 80
20	45	55	1 25	90	2 05	125	2 80
21	50	56	1 25	91	2 05	126	2 85
22	50	57	1 30	92	2 05	127	2 85
23	50	58	1 30	93	2 10	128	2 90
24	55	59	1 35	94	2 10	129	2 90
25	55	60	1 35	95	2 15	130	2 95
26	60	61	1 40	96	2 15	131	2 95
27	60	62	1 40	97	2 20	132	2 95
28	65	63	1 40	98	2 20	133	3 00
29	65	64	1 45	99	2 25	134	3 00
30	70	65	1 45	100	2 25	135	3 05
31	70	66	1 50	101	2 30	136	3 05
32	70	67	1 50	102	2 30	137	3 10
33	75	68	1 55	103	2 30	138	3 10
34	75	69	1 55	104	2 35	139	3 15
35	80	70	1 60	105	2 35	140	3 15

Miles.	Fare.	Miles.	Fare.	Miles.	Fare.	Miles.	Fare.
	$ cts.		$ cts.		$ cts.		$ cts.
141	3 20	185	4 15	229	5 15	273	6 15
142	3 20	186	4 20	230	5 20	274	6 15
143	3 20	187	4 20	231	5 20	275	6 20
144	3 25	188	4 25	232	5 20	276	6 20
145	3 25	189	4 25	233	5 25	277	6 25
146	3 30	190	4 30	234	5 25	278	6 25
147	3 30	191	4 30	235	5 30	279	6 30
148	3 35	192	4 30	236	5 30	280	6 30
149	3 35	193	4 35	237	5 35	281	6 35
150	3 40	194	4 35	238	5 35	282	6 35
151	3 40	195	4 40	239	5 40	283	6 35
152	3 40	196	4 40	240	5 40	284	6 40
153	3 45	197	4 45	241	5 45	285	6 40
154	3 45	198	4 45	242	5 45	286	6 45
155	3 50	199	4 50	243	5 45	287	6 45
156	3 50	200	4 50	244	5 50	288	6 50
157	3 55	201	4 55	245	5 50	289	6 50
158	3 55	202	4 55	246	5 55	290	6 55
159	3 60	203	4 55	247	5 55	291	6 55
160	3 60	204	4 60	248	5 60	292	6 55
161	3 65	205	4 60	249	5 60	293	6 60
162	3 65	206	4 65	250	5 65	294	6 60
163	3 65	297	4 65	251	5 65	295	6 65
164	3 70	208	4 70	252	5 65	296	6 65
165	3 70	209	4 70	253	5 70	297	6 70
166	3 75	210	4 75	254	5 70	298	6 70
167	3 75	211	4 75	255	5 75	299	6 75
168	3 80	212	4 75	256	5 75	300	6 75
169	3 80	213	4 80	257	5 80	301	6 80
170	3 85	214	4 80	258	5 80	302	6 80
171	3 85	215	4 85	259	5 85	303	6 80
172	3 85	216	4 85	260	5 85	304	6 85
173	3 90	217	4 90	261	5 90	305	6 85
174	3 90	218	4 90	262	5 90	306	6 90
175	3 95	219	4 95	263	5 90	307	6 90
176	3 95	220	4 95	264	5 95	308	6 95
177	4 00	221	5 00	265	5 95	309	6 95
178	4 00	222	5 00	266	6 00	310	7 00
179	4 05	223	5 00	267	6 00	311	7 00
180	4 05	224	5 05	268	6 05	312	7 00
181	4 10	225	5 05	269	6 05	313	7 05
182	4 10	226	5 10	270	6 10	314	7 05
183	4 10	227	5 10	271	6 10	315	7 10
184	4 15	228	5 15	272	6 10	316	7 10

Miles.	Fare.	Miles.	Fare.	Miles.	Fare.	Miles.	Fare.
	$ cts.		$ cts.		$ cts.		$ cts.
317	7 15	338	7 60	359	8 10	380	8 55
318	7 15	339	7 65	360	8 10	381	8 60
319	7 20	340	7 65	361	8 15	382	8 60
320	7 20	341	7 70	362	8 15	383	8 60
321	7 25	342	7 70	363	8 15	384	8 65
322	7 25	343	7 70	364	8 20	385	8 65
323	7 25	344	7 75	365	8 20	386	8 70
324	7 30	345	7 75	366	8 25	387	8 70
325	7 30	346	7 80	367	8 25	388	8 75
326	7 35	347	7 80	368	8 30	389	8 75
327	7 35	348	7 85	369	8 30	390	8 80
328	7 40	349	7 85	370	8 35	391	8 80
329	7 40	350	7 90	371	8 35	392	8 80
330	7 45	351	7 90	372	8 35	393	8 85
331	7 45	352	7 90	373	8 40	394	8 85
332	7 45	353	7 95	374	8 40	395	8 90
333	7 50	354	7 95	375	8 45	396	8 90
334	7 50	355	8 00	376	8 45	397	8 95
335	7 55	356	8 00	377	8 50	398	8 95
336	7 55	357	8 05	378	8 50	399	9 00
337	7 60	358	8 05	379	8 55	400	9 00

In effect May 1st, 1888.   No charge less than 25 cents.

Where 1st Class Unlimited Passenger Rate is From	To	Excess Rate will be per 100 lbs.	Where 1st Class Unlimited Passenger Rate is From	To	Excess Rate will be per 100 lbs.	Where 1st Class Unlimited Passenger Rate is From	To	Excess Rate will be per 100 lbs.
$ cts.	$ cts.	$ cts.	$ cts.	$ cts.	$ cts.	$ cts.	$ cts.	$ cts.
05..	60..	15	17 51..17 95..		2 15	34 21..34 60..		4 15
61..	85..	20	17 96..18 35..		2 20	34 61. 35 00..		4 20
86..	1 10..	25	18 36..18 75..		2 25	35 01....' 45..		4 25
1 11..	1 40..	30	18 76..19 20..		2 30	35 46..35 85..		4 30
1 41..	1 70..	35	19 21..19 60..		2 35	35 86..36 25..		4 35
1 71..	2 00..	40	19 61..20 00..		2 40	36 26..36 70..		4 40
2 01..	2 40..	45	20 01..20 45..		2 45	36 71..37 10..		4 45
2 41..	2 80..	50	20 46..20 85..		2 50	37 11..37 50..		4 50
2 81..	3 25..	55	20 86..21 25..		2 55	37 51..37 95..		4 55
3 26..	3 75..	60	21 26..21 70..		2 60	37 96..38 35..		4 60
3 76..	4 35..	65	21 71..22 10..		2 65	38 36..38 75..		4 65
4 36..	5 00..	70	22 11..22 50..		2 70	38 76..39 20..		4 70
5 01..	5 80..	75	22 51..22 95..		2 75	39 21..39 60..		4 75
5 81..	6 70..	80	22 96..23 35..		2 80	39 61..40 00..		4 80
6 71..	7 10..	85	23 36..23 75..		2 85	40 01..40 45..		4 85
7 11..	7 50..	90	23 76..24 20..		2 90	40 46..40 85..		4 90
7 51..	7 95..	95	24 21..24 60..		2 95	40 86..41 25..		4 95
7 96..	8 35..	1 00	24 61..25 00..		3 00	41 26..41 70..		5 00
8 36..	8 75..	1 05	25 01..25 45..		3 05	41 71..42 10..		5 05
8 76..	9 20..	1 10	25 46..25 85..		3 10	42 11..42 50..		5 10
9 21..	9 60..	1 15	25 86. 26 25..		3 15	42 51..42 95.		5 15
9 61..10 00..		1 20	26 26..26 70.		3 20	42 96..43 35..		5 20
10 01..10 45..		1 25	26 71..27 10..		3 25	43 36..43 75..		5 25
10 46..10 85..		1 30	27 11..27 50..		3 30	43 76..44 20..		5 30
10 86..11 25..		1 35	27 51..27 95..		3 35	44 21..44 60..		5 35
11 26..11 70..		1 40	27 96..28 35..		3 40	44 61..45 00..		5 40
11 71..12 10..		1 45	28 36..28 75..		3 45	45 01..45 45..		5 45
12 11..12 50..		1 50	28 76..29 20..		3 50	45 46..45 85..		5 50
12 51..12 95..		1 55	29 21..29 60..		3 55	45 86..46 25..		5 55
12 96..13 35..		1 60	29 61..30 00..		3 60	46 26..46 70..		5 60
13 36..13 75..		1 65	30 01..30 45..		3 65	46 71..47 10..		5 65
13 76..14 20..		1 70	30 46..30 85..		3 70	47 11..47 50..		5 70
14 21..14 60..		1 75	30 86..31 25..		3 75	47 51..47 95..		5 75
14 61..15 00..		1 80	31 26..31 70..		3 80	47 96..48 35..		5 80
15 01..15 45..		1 85	31 71..32 10..		3 85	48 36..48 75..		5 85
15 46..15 85..		1 90	32 11..32 50..		3 90	48 76..49 20..		5 90
15 86..16 25..		1 95	32 51..32 95..		3 95	49 21..49 60..		5 95
16 26..16 70..		2 00	32 96..33 35..		4 00	49 61..50 00..		6 00
16 71. 17 10..		2 05	33 36..33 75..		4 05	50 01..50 45..		6 05
17 11..17 50..		2 10	33 76..34 26..		4 10	50 46..50 85..		6 10

Where 1st Class Unlimited Passenger Rate is		Excess Rate will be per 100 lbs.	Where 1st Class Unlimited Passenger Rate is		Excess Rate will be per 100 lbs.	Where 1st Class Unlimited Passenger Rate is		Excess Rate will be per 100 lbs.
From	To		From	To		From	To	
$ cts.	$ cts.	$ cts.	$ cts.	$ cts.	$ cts.	$ cts.	$ cts.	$ cts.
50 86	52 25	6 15	67 51	67 95	8 15	84 01	84 45	10 15
51 26	51 70	6 20	67 96	68 35	8 20	84 46	84 85	10 20
51 71	52 10	6 25	68 36	68 75	8 25	84 86	85 25	10 25
52 11	52 50	6 30	68 76	69 20	8 30	85 26	85 70	10 30
52 51	52 95	6 35	69 21	69 60	8 35	85 71	86 10	10 35
52 96	53 35	6 40	69 61	70 00	8 40	86 11	86 45	10 40
53 36	53 75	6 45	70 01	70 45	8 45	86 46	86 85	10 45
53 76	54 20	6 50	70 46	70 85	8 50	86 86	87 25	10 50
54 21	54 60	6 55	70 86	71 25	8 55	87 26	87 70	10 55
54 61	55 00	6 60	71 26	71 70	8 60	87 71	88 10	10 60
55 01	55 45	6 65	71 71	72 10	8 65	88 11	88 45	10 65
55 46	55 85	6 70	72 11	72 45	8 70	88 46	88 85	10 70
55 86	56 25	6 75	72 46	72 85	8 75	88 86	89 25	10 75
56 26	56 70	6 80	72 86	73 25	8 80	89 26	89 70	10 80
56 71	57 10	6 85	73 26	73 70	8 85	89 71	90 10	10 85
57 11	57 50	6 90	73 71	74 10	8 90	90 11	90 50	10 90
57 51	57 95	6 95	74 11	74 45	8 95	90 51	90 90	10 95
57 96	58 35	7 00	74 46	74 85	9 00	90 91	91 30	11 00
58 36	58 75	7 05	74 86	75 25	9 05	91 31	91 70	11 05
58 76	59 20	7 10	75 26	75 70	9 10	91 71	92 15	11 10
59 21	59 60	7 15	75 71	76 10	9 15	92 16	92 60	11 15
59 61	60 00	7 20	76 11	76 45	9 20	92 61	93 05	11 20
60 01	60 45	7 25	76 46	76 85	9 25	93 06	93 45	11 25
60 46	60 85	7 30	76 86	77 25	9 30	93 46	93 90	11 30
60 86	61 25	7 35	77 26	77 70	9 35	93 91	94 30	11 35
61 26	61 70	7 40	77 71	78 10	9 40	94 31	94 75	11 40
61 71	62 10	7 45	78 11	78 45	9 45	94 76	95 20	11 45
62 11	62 50	7 50	78 46	78 85	9 50	95 21	95 65	11 50
62 51	62 95	7 55	78 86	79 25	9 55	95 66	96 10	11 55
62 96	63 35	7 60	79 26	79 70	9 60	96 11	96 50	11 60
63 36	63 75	7 65	79 71	80 10	9 65	96 51	96 95	11 65
63 76	64 20	7 70	80 11	80 50	9 70	96 96	97 40	11 70
64 21	64 60	7 75	80 51	80 95	9 75	97 41	97 85	11 75
64 61	65 00	7 80	80 96	81 40	9 80	97 86	98 25	11 80
65 01	65 45	7 85	81 41	81 85	9 85	98 26	98 65	11 85
65 46	65 85	7 90	81 86	82 30	9 90	98 66	99 05	11 90
65 86	66 25	7 95	82 31	82 75	9 95	99 06	99 45	11 95
66 26	66 70	8 00	82 76	83 15	10 00	99 46	99 85	12 00
66 71	67 10	8 05	83 16	83 60	10 05	99 86	100 25	12 05
67 11	67 50	8 10	83 61	84 00	10 10	100 26	100 65	12 10

Charge 12 per cent. of first class unlimited fare if over $100 65.

STEAMBOAT ARRANGEMENTS.

I.—The following steamship companies allow to travelling members of the Association 300 lbs. of baggage free, and deduct 25 per cent. off regular passenger fares, viz. :

Boston, Halifax and P.E. Line.
Bras D'Or Steam Navigation Company.
Fiswick's Line.
Humphrey Steamship Line.
International Steamship Company.
Muskoka and Nipissing Navigation Co.—Lakes Muskoka, Rosseau and Joseph. Georgian Bay. Maganettawan Waters.
Niagara Navigation Co.—Strs. Chippewa, Cibola, and Chicora. (Book tickets, 20 round trips, $8.00.)
Toronto and St. Catharines—Steamer Garden City. (Book tickets, 10 round trips, $5.00.)
Nova Scotia Steamship Company.
Toronto, Port Dalhousie and St. Catharines.—Strs. Empress of India and Garden City. (Book tickets, 10 round trips, $5.00.)
Toronto and Hamilton.—Steamers Macassa and Modjeska. Fare from Toronto to Hamilton, 60 cents ; 300 lbs. baggage. (Book tickets, 10 round trips, $5.00.)
Toronto and Rochester.—Steamer Carmona.
Bay Quinte Railway Navigation Company.
Deseronto and Napanee Line.—Steamer Pilgrim.
Deseronto and Picton Line.—Steamers Deseronto and Quinte.
Trenton, Belleville and Picton Line.—Steamer Quinte.
Deseronto, Picton, Kingston and Ogdensburg.—Str. Armenia.
P. E. Island S. S. Navigation Co.
Quebec Gulf Ports S. S. Co.

Union Line Bay and River Steamers.—All points on St. John River.

The Clement's Line of Steamers allow 20 per cent. off regular fares and 300 lbs. of baggage free.

Yarmouth Steamship Co.—From Yarmouth, St. John and Boston, and *vice versa.*

Charlottetown Steam Navigation C '.

Boston, Halifax & Prince Edward Island.

Canada Atlantic Steamship Co.

Halifax & Prince Edward Island.

Anglo French Steamship Co.

II.—Ottawa and Montreal Navigation Co.—Ottawa to Montreal and *vice versa,* $2.50 each way, and 300 lbs. of baggage free. Tickets to be had at Company's offices at Montreal and Ottawa.

III.—Richelieu and Ontario Navigation Co.—Montreal to Toronto and *vice versa,* $8.00 each way, and 300 lbs. of baggage free. Members' wives same privileges.

North Shore Navigation Co. of Ontario, Ltd.—Strs. City of Midland, City of Collingwood, City of London, Favorite, Manitou.

NORTH-WESTERN TRANSPORTATION CO.'s STEAMERS.
SARNIA LINE.

For rates apply to Secretary of C. T. A., or P. S. Slatter, Grand Trunk Railway, cor. King and Yonge Streets, Toronto.

CANADIAN PACIFIC STEAMSHIP CO.

For rates apply to Secretary, C.T.A., or W. R. Callaway, District Passenger Agent, Canadian Pacific Railway, cor. King and Yonge Streets, Toronto.

NORTHERN TRANSIT COMPANY, COLLINGWOOD.

Stop-over Tickets, 300 lbs. baggage free. Steamers Atlantic, Northern Belle and Pacific, to Killarney, Manitowaning, Little Current, Mudge Bay, Gore Bay, Spanish River, Algoma Mills, Cockburn Island, Thessalon, Bruce Mines, Hilton, Blind River, St. Joseph's Island, Garden River, Sault Ste. Marie.

SPECIAL ARRANGEMENTS.

BOOK TICKETS.

Niagara Navigation Co.—Steamers Chippewa, Cibola and Chicora. Book tickets, 20 round trips, $8.00.

Hamilton Navigation Co.—Steamers Modjeska and Macassa. Book tickets, 10 round trips, $5.00.

Empress of India to Port Dalhousie. Book tickets, 20 round trips, $8.00.

Toronto and St. Catharines—Steamer Garden City. Book tickets, 10 round trips, $5.00, to be obtained from H. W. Van Every. Office, Toronto Arcade, Yonge st.

For the convenience of members and their families, any of the above can be obtained at the Secretary's Office, 51 Yonge Street, or A. F. Webster, corner Yonge and King Streets, and Chas. E. Burns, 77 Yonge Street, Toronto.

Niagara Falls Park and River Railway (Electric Road)—Special Rates have been made for Queenston, Niagara Falls, Chippewa and Buffalo, to be had at the Office of the Secretary, 51 Yonge Street, W. S. Duffield, Sanford Manufacturing Co., Hamilton, and the office of the Company, Niagara Falls.

MARITIME PROVINCES.

Members going to the above Provinces and wishing to return to Montreal or Toronto via Portland or Boston, can do so by Yarmouth Steamship Co. or International Steamship Co., having baggage bonded through. Full information to be obtained from C. E. McPherson, C.P.R. Office, St. John, N.B., or C. McLauchlan, St. John, N.B.

ACT OF INCORPORATION

AND AMENDMENTS THERETO.

An Act to Incorporate the COMMERCIAL TRAVELLERS'
ASSOCIATION OF CANADA.

37 Vic., Cap. 96 (Dom.)

Whereas an Association under the name of "THE COM-
MERCIAL TRAVELLERS' ASSOCIATION OF CANADA," has existed for some time past in the city of Toronto, having for
its object the moral, intellectual, and financial improvement and advancement and welfare of its members ; and
whereas the members of the said Association have prayed
to be incorporated with certain powers, and it is expedient
to grant their petition : Therefore, Her Majesty, by and
with the advice and consent of the Senate and House of
Commons of Canada, enacts as follows :

1. Warring Kennedy, William J. Bryan, Robert J.
Wylie, James Patterson, and William L. MacGillivray,
and the other present members of the said Association,
and all other persons who may hereafter become members
of the corporation hereby created, shall be, and they are
hereby constituted, a body politic and corporate in fact
and in name, under the name of "The Commercial Travellers' Association of Canada," having its headquarters in
the city of Toronto ; and by that name shall have power
from time to time, and at any time hereafter, to purchase,
acquire, possess, hold, exchange, accept and receive, for
themselves and their successors, all lands, tenements, and
hereditaments, and all real or immovable estate being
and situated in the Dominion of Canada, necessary for
the actual use and occupation of the said corporation, and
the said property to hypothecate, sell, alienate and dispose
of, and to acquire other instead thereof for the same pur-

poses; and any majority of the said corporation, for the time being, shall have full power and authority to make and establish such rules, regulations and by-laws, in no respect inconsistent with this Act nor with the laws then in force in the Dominion of Canada, as they may deem expedient and necessary for the interest of the said Corporation, and for the admission of members thereof, and the same, as also such by-laws and regulations of the Association as may be in force at the passing of this Act, to amend and repeal, from time to time, in whole or in part.

2. All the revenues of the Corporation, from whatever source they may be derived, shall be devoted to the maintenance and objects of the Corporation, to the providing and furnishing of libraries and reading-rooms, and for the purchase of books, periodicals and newspapers for the said libraries and reading-rooms, as the directors of the said Association may decide, for the benefit of the members of the said Corporation, and for the erection and repair of the buildings necessary for the purposes of the said Corporation, and for the payment of expenses legitimately incurred in carrying out any of the objects above referred to. Provided always that it shall be lawful for the Board of Directors of the said Corporation to invest the funds of the said Corporation in the bonds and debentures of any incorporated company transacting business in any of the Provinces of the Dominion, or of any Municipal Corporation in Canada, or on mortgage of real estate, or in any Government securities of the Dominion, or any Province thereof, or in the stock of any chartered Bank of Canada.

Note—This section was amended by 45 Vic., cap. 120, sec. 5, post.

3. The affairs and business of the said Corporation shall by managed by an Executive Committee, or Board of Directors, composed of the officers of the said Corporation, consisting of a President, seven Vice-Presidents, a Secretary and a Treasurer, and twenty-eight other members of the Corporation.

4. All real and personal estate, at present the property of the said Association, or which may hereafter be acquired by the Corporation now constituted, or by the members

thereof, in their capacity as such, by purchase, gift, de-
vise, or otherwise, and all debts, claims and rights, which
they may be, or become possessed of in such capacity, are
hereby declared to be the property of the Corporation
constituted by this Act, and the said Corporation shall be
chargeable with and liable for all the debts, liabilities, and
obligations of the said Association, and the rules, regulations and by-laws now established for the management of
the said Association, or for the management of the reading-rooms and libraries above referred to, shall be, and
continue to be the rules, regulations and by laws of the
said Corporation, until altered or repealed, in the manner
prescribed by this Act.

5. Until others are elected, according to the by-laws of
the Corporation, the present officers of the said Association shall be the officers of the Corporation, that is to say,
the said Warring Kennedy shall be President, the said W.
J. Bryan, R. J. Wylie and Andrew Robertson, James
Cantlie, Adam Brown, W. E. Sanford, and John Burrill
shall be the Vice-Presidents, and the said James Patterson
shall be the Treasurer, the said W. L. MacGillivray shall be
the Secretary, Charles Riley, Robert Cuthbert, W. Norris,
J. Fairbairn, J. F. Ellis, R. B. Linton, J. B. Mather, D.
McCall, S. Caldecott, James Cooper, Andrew Jack, John
McDougall, James O'Brien, Jacob Wilson, Walter Won-
ham, S. O. Shorey, James Turner, John Brown, Thomas
Christie, Wm. McGivern, Alex. Harvie, John McKenzie,
A. T. Wood, J. H. Park, Edward Long, George Laing,
John Sutherland, and Robert Waddell, the other mem-
bers of the Board of Directors.

6. The general meetings of the said Corporation shall
be held in such manner, after such notice, upon such requisition, and at such times, in the city of Toronto, as
provided by the by-laws of the Corporation.

7. All subscriptions and penalties due to the Corporation, under any by-law, may be recovered by action
or suit in the name of the Corporation, in any court
of competent jurisdiction, but any member may
withdraw from the said Association, at any time,
on payment of all amounts by him due to the Cor-

poration, inclusive of his subscription for the year then current, after which he shall have no claim or demand of any kind against the Corporation.

8. The Corporation shall, at all times, when required so to do by the Governor or the Parliament of Canada, make a full return of all their property, real and personal, and of their receipts and expenditure for such period, and with such details and other information as the Governor, or as Parliament may require.

(Assented to 26th May, 1874.)

An Act to Amend the Act to Incorporate "THE COMMERCIAL TRAVELLERS' ASSOCIATION OF CANADA."

39 VIC., CAP. 68 (Dom.)

WHEREAS by the Act to incorporate "THE COMMERCIAL TRAVELLERS' ASSOCIATION OF CANADA," it was declared that the said Association had for its objects the moral, intellectual, and financial improvement, advancement, and welfare of its members ; and whereas one purpose of the said Association was to insure its members against accidents ; and doubts have been expressed whether such purpose falls by legal construction within the objects so defined ; Therefore, Her Majesty, by and with the advice and consent of the Senate and House of Commons of Canada, declares and enacts as follows :

1. The said Association shall have and has power and authority, with and out of the funds thereof, to make contracts of insurance with any Accident Insurance Company, against accidents or casualties arising to the members of the said Association, whereby they may suffer loss, or injury, or be disabled, or die, and also to apply its funds, from time to time, in benefits, or bonuses, to members thereof, during sickness or disability from accident, casualty, or otherwise, or at death, to the families or personal representatives of such members, and to make, and from time to time to alter such by-laws, rules, and regulations as may be necessar_   ` `` any such purpose.

2. And it is hereby declared that the Association has power and authority to grant any sum of money to the family or representatives of any of the members of the Association who have died by reason of any accident since the incorporation of the said Association, or to grant any sum of money to any of the members of the said Association who are living, but have suffered loss or injury, or have been disabled since the incorporation of the said Associati̇ ɔi.

3. At any annual meeting of the Association, members may vote by proxy, in the election of officers, in such manner as shall be provided by by-law.

(Assented to 12th April, 1876.)

An Act respecting "THE COMMERCIAL TRAVELLERS' ASSO-CIATION OF CANADA."

45 VIC., CAP. 120 (Dom.)

WHEREAS by the Act incorporating the Commercial Travellers' Association of Canada, it is declared that the said Association had for its objects the moral, intellectual, and financial improvement, advancement and welfare of its members ; and whereas by the Act to amend the said Act it was expressly provided that the said Association should have power to apply its funds from time to time in "benefits" or "bonuses" to members thereof, during sickness or disability from accident, casualty or otherwise, or at death to the families or personal representatives of such members ; and whereas shortly after the passing of the said Act the said Association passed by-laws making provision for the payment of bonuses upon the death of a member through accident, and also for a weekly indemnity if disabled, and such By-laws are still in force and have tended to advance the usefulness of the said Association ; and whereas the said Association at its last annual meeting passed By-laws amending their former By-laws, and establishing a "mortuary benefit," to be payable upon the death of a member under the circumstances therein mentioned to his beneficiary or personal representatives; and whereas doubts may arise as to the powers of the Association to pass such "mortuary" By-laws, and it is in the interests of the Association, and expedient that all such doubts should be removed; and whereas the said "bonuses" and "benefits" are in fact intended to afford assistance to the beneficiaries and families of the members, and it is desirable that such intention should be assured and given effect to; and whereas the Association is also desirous that provision should be made for depositing a certain sum with the Receiver-General as a guarantee for the carrying out of the said By-laws; and whereas it is expedient also that changes should be made as to the mode of investment of the funds of the Association; and whereas a petition has been presented praying for the passing of an Act for the above purposes, and it is expedient to grant the prayer of the said petition:

Therefore Her Majesty by and with the advice and consent of the Senate and House of Commons of Canada enacts as follows:

1. The By-laws of the said Association, set forth in the schedule to this Act, shall have the force and effect intended by them, as if expressly enacted by the Parliament of Canada.

2. The "accident bonus" and "mortuary benefit" provided for by the said By-laws shall be respectively payable as therein provided.

3. In the event of the decease of any beneficiary named in any application for membership or renewal thereof, the member by whom such beneficiary was named shall be entitled to have another beneficiary substituted so often as such an event shall occur; and should no new beneficiary be named, the interest of such deceased beneficiary shall survive to any other beneficiary or beneficiaries mentioned in such application or renewal; and should there be none such, the said "bonus" or "benefit" shall be payable to the personal representative of the said member as if no beneficiary had been named.

4. Where more than one beneficiary is named in the application for membership of any member or renewal

thereof, and no apportionment is made therein, such beneficiaries shall share equally in the said "bonus" or "benefit."

5. Section two of the Act passed in the 37th year of Her Majesty's reign, chaptered 96, is hereby amended by striking out the words " in the stock of any chartered bank of Canada," and by inserting in lieu thereof, the words "by depositing the said funds or any part thereof with any chartered bank or loan company in Canada upon receiving an undertaking or deposit receipt therefor from such bank or company."

6. The Association shall, on or before the first of July next, deposit with the Receiver-General the sum of fifty thousand dollars, as security for the fulfilment of the purposes and objects provided by the said By-laws, and for securing to members and beneficiaries the payment of such sum or sums of money as may under the provisions of this Act, and the By-laws of the Association, become payable to them ; and no portion thereof shall be withdrawn, except with the sanction of the Governor in Council on report of the Treasury Board.

7. The said sum may consist of money or of any of the securities mentioned in the Act incorporating the Association, as amended by this Act (excepting mortgages), and the value thereof shall be estimated by the Receiver-General according to their market value at the time of such deposit.

8. The Association may from time to time deposit with the Receiver-General any further sum or sums of money or securities, for the purposes and objects provided by the said By-laws ; and so much of such deposits as may be necessary from time to time to meet the requirements of the said By-laws shall be payable, or securities to the like amount shall be delivered up to the Association by the Receiver-General, on requisition therefor, from time to time made under the seal of the Association, and the respective signatures of the President, Secretary and Treasurer, and counter-signature of one of the Auditors of the Association.

9. The interest upon securities forming such deposits

shall be payable to the Association as it falls due and is received.

10. The By-laws set forth in the schedule to this Act may be amended by the said Association, as provided by its Act of Incorporation and By-laws ; but subject always to the approval of the Governor in Council, and so that the said amendments are not contrary to anything in this Act contained.

(Assented to 17th May, 1882.)

NOTE.—The By-laws in the schedule are No. 16, 17, 18, 19, 65, (a) (b) (c) 66, 67, (a) (b) (c) (d) 68, (a) (b) 69, 70, 71, 72, 73, 74, 75, 76, 77, 78. hereinafter set out as amended, 30th December, 1886, and approved by the Governor in Council by order, dated 30th June, 1887.

An Act relating to " THE COMMERCIAL TRAVELLERS' ASSOCIATION OF CANADA."

46 VIC., CAP. 61 (Ont.)

Whereas the Commercial Travellers' Association of Canada, under the several Acts of the Parliament of Canada relating thereto, passed By-laws making provision for the payment out of its funds of "Accident Bonuses," and "Mortuary Benefits," to the members of the Association and their families ; and whereas such By-laws were confirmed by an Act of the said Parliament, passed at its last session and chaptered one hundred and twenty, and it is expedient that the benefits under such By-laws should be assured and given effect to, so far as the same is within the power of the Legislature of Ontario ;

Therefore, Her Majesty, by and with the advice and consent of the legislative Assembly of the Province of Ontario, enacts as follows :

1. So far as the same is within the power of the Legislature of Ontario, it is hereby declared and provided that when, under the By-laws of the said Association, any money becomes payable to, or for the use or benefit of any member thereof, such money shall be free from all claims by the creditors of such member; and where, on the death

of any member of the said Association, any sum of money becomes payable under such By-laws, the same shall be paid by the Association, or the proper officers thereof, to the person or persons entitled thereto under the said By-laws ; and such money shall, to the extent of three thousand dollars, and when the same is payable to the wife or child, or children of the deceased member or any of them, be free from all claims by the personal representatives or creditors of the deceased ; and in case any sum is paid in good faith to the person who appears to the Association to be entitled to receive the same, no action shall be brought against the Association, or any officer thereof, in respect to the money so paid ; but, nevertheless, if it subsequently appears that such money has been paid to the wrong person, or persons, the person entitled thereto may recover the amount, with interest, from the person or persons who may have wrongfully received the same.

(Assented to 1st Feb., 1883.)

BY-LAWS.

In the year 1871 a number of the Commercial Travellers of Canada became convinced that a compact or organization of those engaged in their particular sphere of mercantile life, could be made productive of desirable results to its members.

In accordance with this belief, a society was formed in the city of Toronto, under the name of "THE COMMERCIAL TRAVELLERS' ASSOCIATION OF CANADA," and the same duly incorporated by Act of Parliament passed 26th May, 1874, and by an amendment thereto granting further privileges in March, 1876.

The originators of the scheme found at first much to discourage them, but by persistence in their efforts, the Association subsequently grew strong both in numbers and influence, and in consequence thereof eventually succeeded not only in making progress towards the moral and social advantages primarily aimed at, but also in securing important material or financial benefits, which the Commercial Travellers separately, or without such organization, could not hope to obtain.

The material or financial benefits consist partly of preferential rates and privileges from Railway, Steamboat, Insurance and Telegraph Companies, or such other parties from whom Commercial Travellers individually could not obtain any concession from ordinary rates.

The facilities for the mutual interchange of valuable information on matters of peculiar interest to Commercial men also form an appreciable benefit to be derived from such organization.

The moral and social objects of the Association are advanced by a better cultivated acquaintance amongst its members, and the more frequent interchange of courtesies occasioned thereby, which also tend to develop a kindly interest in each other's welfare by those whose occupation necessarily removes them so much from the immediate influences of their homes.

A stated place of general meeting, with Reading Room and Library, also an organ of public expression, are amongst the aims of this Association, as it is believed that such agencies may be made conducive to the intellectual advancement and general social progress of its members.

*Note.—As to By laws prefixed * or * * see note to By-law 91.*

ARTICLE I.—NAME

1. The Association shall be called and known as "THE COMMERCIAL TRAVELLERS' ASSOCIATION OF CANADA."

ARTICLE II.—MEMBERS.

2. The membership shall consist of " Commercial Travellers," hereafter defined, who shall be "Travelling Members," and others hereafter alluded to, who shall be known as " Honorary Members."

ARTICLE III.—OFFICERS.

3. The officers of the Association shall be a President, seven Vice-Presidents, a Secretary and a Treasurer.

4. There shall be an executive Committee, otherwise called the Board of Directors, which shall consist of the above-named officers and twenty-eight other members of the Association.

ARTICLE IV.—DEFINITION OF ELIGIBILITY AND QUALIFICATIONS FOR MEMBERSHIP.

5. A " Commercial Traveller " means primarily and strictly a person who travels to sell merchandise, and the term is more particularly defined in reference to the membership of this Association, as a man, whether Employer or Employee, who travels statedly as salesman for a wholesale business to take orders from dealers or manufacturers for goods which shall be sent afterwards.

6. Applicants for travelling membership in this Association, and who fulfil the above definition, require also the following qualifications, viz.:

7. To travel at least four months in the year in Canada.

8. To have residence or business connection or at least an office in Canada.

9. Not to be indebted to this Association, except for assistance rendered.

10. Not to have been expelled from membership by any Commercial Travellers' Association in Canada, for any offence involving a breach of faith with any Company giving privileges to this Association, or not to have been refused membership by any such Association on grounds other than the mere absence for the time of some of the above qualifications shown in By-laws 5, 6, 7, 8 and 9.

11. To have the approval of the Board of Directors, and to be considered by them not only as eligible and qualified, but also desirable as Members of the Association.

12. The following is a list of the lines of wholesale businesses usually accepted as entitling Travelling Salesmen therefor, to be eligible for Travelling Membership :

Books and Stationery,	Metals,
Boots and Shoes,	Millinery and Laces,
Carpets and Oilcloths,	Organs and Pianos,
Crockery and Glassware,	Optical Goods,
Carriage Furnishings,	Paints and Oils,
Confectionery,	Paper,
Drugs and Chemicals,	Rope and Cordage, [ery,
Dry Goods and Clothing,	Smallwares and Haberdash-
Fancy Goods,	Soaps and Candles,
Groceries,	Sewing Machines,
Hardware,	Tobacco and Cigars,
Hats, Caps and Furs,	Vinegars and Spices,
Jewelry, [Goods,	Wines and Liquors,
Leather and Leather	Wooden Ware.

13. The Directors, however, may entertain applications from duly qualified Commercial Travellers, whose business may not be indicated in any of the above named lines ; but peddlers or those who travel to sell to consumers in any line of business are not qualified or eligible for membership in this Association.

B

ARTICLE V.—MEMBERSHIP.

14. Applicants for Travelling Membership are required to fill up form No. 1, to have the same signed and vouched for by two Directors, also by the Firm represented, when practicable.

15. Persons who have been members may rejoin at any time within the year next succeeding the expiration of the year during any portion of which they were members, provided that they possess the requisite qualifications and fill out and sign form No. 3. Re-admission into the Association will, however, at any time, be conditional on continued eligibility, qualification, and approval by the Board of Directors.

ARTICLE VI.—HONORARY MEMBERS.

16. * * Travelling members of five or more consecutive years' standing, who may have ceased to be Commercial Travellers, shall be eligible as Honorary Members, and on becoming such, shall be entitled to all the rights and privileges of members, except travelling privileges ; provided always, that application for such honorary membership shall be made within twelve months after the applicant shall have ceased to be a travelling member; and provided also, that those who fail to make application as aforesaid, and also those who are, or may hereafter be Honorary Members, but fail to rejoin, as permitted by By-law 15, shall cease to be eligible as Honorary Members.

17. * Applicants for Honorary Membership are required to fill up Form No. 2, such application to be subject to the approval of the Board of Directors, as well as all other conditions affecting membership, and which are not essentially peculiar to travelling members.

18. *Honorary Members becoming eligible, and qualified for travelling membership, may become such on complying with the requirements of applicants for such membership.

ARTICLE VII.—SUBSCRIPTIONS.

19. *The Annual Subscription for members shall be ten dollars, to be deposited with the application for membership.

20. Certificates of Membership are not transferable under any circumstances whatever.

21. In the event of a certificate being lost, and a duplicate to replace it being required, the sum of two dollars shall be paid for the same; and any member finding a lost Certificate is expected to send it immediately to the Secretary of the Association, at Toronto.

22. Annual Subscription shall be for Membership to the end of the current year in which Membership is obtained.

23. Benefits and Bonuses expire by date at twelve o'clock, midnight, on the 31st of December.

24. The Directors and Officers elect are required to pay the Annual Fees before taking their seats as Directors at the Board meetings of the Association, in the year for which they are elected.

25. Any Secretary of the Association who is authorized to issue Certificates of Membership shall have the discretionary power of doing so at once, to qualified applicants, when he fully believes they will be approved of, but in cases where he has reason to doubt such approval, he shall not issue the Certificates, but shall hold over the applications, pending the approval of the Board of Directors, to whom he shall communicate his knowledge and views of the circumstances of the applicants as regards qualifications, eligibility, and other considerations.

26. All candidates, upon being admitted members of the Association, are required, when practicable, to sign the Constitution and By-laws in a book kept by the Secretary for that purpose.

27. It shall be the duty of every member of the Association to report to the Secretary any matter coming under his cognizance, which may in any way affect the interests, character, or prospects of the Association, and any irregularity on the part of its members, or others, which would

affect the interests of any Railway or other Company from whom this Association has special privileges.

28. Certificates of membership, issued by the Secretary of the Association through dece_{ption} or misrepresentation on the part of the applicants, and such Certificates as do not pass the approval of the Board of Directors, may be at once recalled or cancelled, in which case the subscription paid shall be returned to the parties, deducting a proportion to be estimated by the Directors, based upon the cost of issue, the investigation of the case, and the value of benefits received meanwhile through such Certificate by the holder thereof.

ARTICLE VIII.—ELECTION OF OFFICERS.

29. Nominations to any office must be restricted to those who are then duly accepted members, and should also be restricted to those who consent to stand as candidates, and who are enabled to give the requisite attendance at the meetings, and to perform the other duties devolving upon them by virtue of the position.

30. The President, Vice-Presidents, Directors and Treasurer shall be elected annually. Should only the requisite number be nominated to fill any office or offices, he or they shall be declared duly elected ; but in the event of more than a sufficient number being nominated, a ballot shall be taken as provided in By-law 57, when the candidate or candidates to a number sufficient to fill such office or offices, receiving the highest number of votes shall be declared duly elected. Should there be a tie upon a vote for any office or upon any motion, the Chairman of the meeting shall have a casting vote.

31. Retiring officers are eligible for re-election if duly nominated.

32. The Secretary of the Association in Toronto shall be a paid officer, and shall be appointed by the Directors. Those who act as Secretaries in other places shall also be appointed by the Board of Directors.

ARTICLE IX.—COMPOSITION OF THE BOARD OF DIRECTORS.

33. The respective quota of Members to be elected to the Board of Directors shall be from, or shall represent, the various places as follows :

34. Toronto—President, Treasurer, First and Second Vice-Presidents, and nine other Directors.

35. Hamilton—Two Vice-Presidents, (who shall be designated for local purposes as First and Second Vice-Presidents) and six other Directors.

36. Montreal — One Vice-President, and two other Directors.

37. Guelph—One Vice-President, and one other Director.

38. Kingston—Two Directors.

39. Victoria, B.C.—Two Directors.

40. Brantford—Two Directors.

41. Winnipeg — One Vice-President, and two other Directors.

42. Berlin—Two Directors.

43. Nominations for the Board of Directors shall be made at the General Meeting to be held on the first Saturday in December without further notice.

44. All vacancies upon the Board or in any office arising from death, resignation, or by absence as hereinafter provided, shall be filled by the Board of Directors, except that the First and Second Vice-Presidents shall succeed respectively to the next highest office, upon any vacancies occurring therein. Should any member of the Toronto *quota* of the Board absent himself for three consecutive regular Board meetings, without previous leave by resolution of the Board having been obtained, his seat shall thereupon become vacant.

ARTICLE X.—DUTIES OF OFFICERS.

45. *Auditors.* There shall be two auditors elected at the annual meeting, whose duties shall be to audit the books and accounts of the Association.

46. The *President* and First *Vice-President* shall be members *ex officio* of all committees. The President shall have general oversight of the affairs of the Association, and shall preside at all meetings ; in his absence the Vice-Presidents, according to seniority, shall perform his duties. In the event of the absence of the President and First and Second Vice-Presidents from any meeting, the meeting

shall have power to organize and appoint a Chairman *pro tem.*

47. The duties of the *Secretary* shall be to attend all meetings in connection with the Association, to take correct minutes of the same, to give all proper notices, to issue certificates of membership, to keep the Books of the Association as may be proper and necessary, to attend promptly to all correspondence under the direction of the President, or in his absence the senior Vice President, to collect and receive all moneys of the Association, and deposit the same forthwith to the credit of the Association in its Bank, to make statements thereof as the Board may require, and generally to conform to the wishes of the B ard. The Secretary shall furnish such guarantee bonds as may be required by the Board for the performance of his duties.

48. It shall be the duty of the *Treasurer* to take charge of the blank certificates of membership, issue them from time to time, as may be necessary, to the Secretary, keeping a book for such purpose, in which the date of issue to the Secretary shall be noted, which book shall be balanced monthly, and the certificates accounted for. He shall also receive all securities or evidences of title belonging to the Association, and forthwith deposit the same. subject to the order of the Board, in the Association's Bank, or in such other place as the Board may appoint for safe keeping.

ARTICLE XI.—BOARD OF DIRECTORS.

49. The Board of Directors shall have the care and superintendence of the Association, and the custody of its property. The Board shall cause to be kept fair and accurate minutes of all their transactions, and of all receipts and payments on account of the Association, and shall cause such accounts to be made up every year, viz.: to the thirtieth of November, and submit the same to the Annual General Meetings of the Association, and all accounts shall be passed by the Directors before being paid.

50. The Board of Directors shall employ so much of the income of the Association as shall appear to them necessary for the promotion of its objects and interests.

51. All payments shall be by cheque upon the Association's Bank, signed by the President and Treasurer, and countersigned by the Secretary ; in the absence of the President, the senior Vice-President shall attach his signature to the cheque.

52. The Board of Directors shall have the power of forming themselves into Sub-Committees, whose decisions, however, shall not be considered as final, until confirmed by the Board.

ARTICLE XII.—MEETINGS.

53. The Board of Directors shall meet on the last Saturday of each month, at two o'clock, p.m., or as often as they may deem necessary for the welfare of the Association—three to form a quorum.

54. A General Meeting of the Association shall be held at their Rooms in Toronto, on the first Saturday in March, June, September and December, at eight o'clock p.m.—ten to form a quorum.

55. The President, or, in his absence, the First Vice-President, shall, at the request of two members of the Board, call a special meeting of the Board of Directors, one day's notice having been given by the Secretary, and no business shall be transacted other than that contained in the notice ; five to form a quorum.

56. Special meetings of the Association shall be called by the President, or, in his absence, by the First Vice-President, at the request of five members, notice of which must be given, at least four days previous to such meetings, either by circular or advertisement in the public press. No business shall be transacted at such meetings other than that stated in the notice.

57. The Annual meeting of the Association shall be held in Toronto, in the last week in December. Ten to form a quorum. Due notice of this meeting shall be given to every member, and a suitable ballot slip, showing the nominations for Officers and Directors of the Association, shall therewith also be sent by mail to each member, requesting him to signify his choice thereon, and return the same, duly signed, to the Secretary, so as to reach him

not later than the morning of the day appointed for the election.

ARTICLE XIII.—RULES OF ORDER AT MEETINGS.

58. As soon as the presiding officer has taken the chair, and a quorum present, the order of procedure shall be as follows :

(a) The reading of the minutes of last meeting ; the consideration of any objections which may be made to any part thereof, and the approval, with or without amendment, as the case may require.

(b) Admission of members.

(c) The receiving and consideration of any report from the Board of Directors.

(d) The receiving and consideration of any report from Special Committees in the order of priority.

(e) The receiving and consideration of accounts and other communications in the hands of the Secretary and Treasurer.

(f) The consideration of unfinished business in order of priority.

(g) New business.

59. No motion shall be offered to the meeting (if the Secretary requires it) otherwise than in writing.

60. No matter or language expressing the will or intention of any meeting, either of the Board of Directors, or of the Association, shall be considered a proper minute, unless introduced by resolution duly moved and seconded.

61. No question or motion shall be put to the meeting unless moved and seconded, and when put, no other motion shall be receivable, unless it be the motion first to adjourn ; second, to lay on the table ; third, to put the previous question ; fourth, to postpone indefinitely; fifth, to postpone to a certain time; sixth, to refer ; or seventh, to amend ; and these several motions, if made, shall have precedence in the order above stated, and the first three thereof shall be decided without debate.

62. When a blank is to be filled, the question shall first be taken on the highest sum or number, or the longest time proposed.

63. Any member intending to speak on a question shall rise in his place and address the chair. Should more than one person rise to speak at the same time, the chairman shall decide which is entitled to the floor.

64. At the Annual meeting the election of officers shall take precedence in these rules of order, after the meeting is formed, except when there are proposed alterations in the By-laws to be discussed, when the meeting may determine which it will take up first.

ARTICLE XIV.—ACCIDENT BONUSES.

65. * In the event of a member of this Association sustaining any bodily injury from an external, violent or accidental cause, and subject to the conditions hereinafter mentioned, and such injury alone shall have caused his death within six months from the happening thereof, the person or persons of the said member's family whom the said member shall name as his beneficiary or beneficiaries in his application for membership, or any renewal thereof, or the legal representative of such deceased member if no such beneficiary or beneficiaries shall have been so named, shall be entitled to the sum of one thousand dollars from the funds of this Association.

(a) * In the event of a member of this Association sustaining any bodily injury which shall not be fatal, but which shall independently of any other cause totally disable him and prevent him from continuing the prosecution of any and every kind of business, then, on satisfactory proof of such injury and disability being furnished to the Secretary, such member shall be compensated from the funds of this Association against loss of time thereby caused, in the sum of five dollars per week, during the continuance of such disability, and for a period not exceeding twenty-six weeks.

(b) ** The provisions of this By-law shall not extend to any bodily injury of which there is no external or visible sign, nor to any bodily injury happening directly or indirectly in consequence of disease, or by the taking of poison, or by any surgical operation, or medical or mechanical treatment for disease, nor to any case except when the injury aforesaid is a proximate and sole cause of the disability or death ; and no claim shall be made under this By-law when the death or injury may have been caused by duelling or fighting, or by suicide (while sane or insane) or self-inflicted injuries (so inflicted with intent to defraud) or by concealed weapons carried by a member in whose regard application for accident bonuses may be made, or when the death or injury may have happened in consequence of war or invasion, or by exposure to any obvious or unnecessary danger (unless in the laudable effort to save human life or property) or while engaged in or in consequence of any unlawful act.

(c) *Any sum of money which may be paid by way of compensation to any member by virtue of this By-law, shall be counted in diminution of the sum which may be payable in the event of death arising from the same accident or injury.

ARTICLE XV.—MORTUARY BENEFITS.

66. * On the death of a member the person or persons of his family whom he shall name in his application for membership, or any renewal thereof, as his beneficiary or beneficiaries, or in default thereof, the legal representative of such member, shall be entitled to receive a benefit as provided in the next succeeding By-law.

67. * The said benefit shall be provided for and ascertained as follows :—

(a) The net funds and investments of the Association, as they were on the fifteenth day of December, one thousand eight hundred and eighty-one, shall be and the same are hereby set apart, and shall be known as the "Permanent Reserve Fund."

(b) ** The interest earned on such Permanent Reserve Fund, and on the current funds of the Association, together with one half of the annual subscriptions from membership fees, made up to the thirtieth day of November in each year (first deducting from such fees all outlays other than those under By-laws 65 and 66), shall be known as the "Annual Benefit Allotment," and shall be for the payment of the said benefit.

(c) **The Directors shall determine annually, as of the thirtieth day of November in each year, under competent advice, a "mortuary benefit" for the ensuing year, and such "mortuary benefit" shall be the result arising by dividing the "annual benefit allotment by the expected mortality of the Association, according to the H. M. Table of Mortality, of the Institute of Actuaries modified from time to time, as far as may be considered prudent by the actual mortality of the Association.

(d) * The "mortuary benefit" thus ascertained shall be the benefit payable under By-law 66.

68. * The benefit under By-laws 66 and 67 shall be and the same is subject to the following provisions, namely—

(a) * The whole amount thereof shall be payable only upon the death of a member who shall have paid his subscriptions, and been a member for ten or more consecutive years immediately preceding his decease, and for this purpose the year in which the death occurs shall be counted as one year, and such benefit shall be reduced one-tenth for each year of consecutive membership less than ten.

(aa) ** Provided also that the amount of such benefit as to persons admitted to membership on and after the 1st day of January, 1887, under By-law 14, and being new members, shall be regulated, as to scale, according to the age of the applicant at his birthday next following the date of his admission, and shall be payable upon the table following : viz :

Age at birthday next following admission.	Proportion of benefit payable.
35 years and under.	The whole benefit.
36 to 40 years inclusive	85 p.c. of whole benefit.
41 to 45 " "	70 " "
46 to 50 " "	55 " "
51 to 55 " "	40 " "
56 to 60 " "	30 " "
61 to 65 " "	20 " "
66 to 70 and over.	15 " "

Subject always to a proportional reduction of one-tenth for each year required to complete the full term of ten consecutive years as required by Sec. (*a*).

(*b*) * Claims arising under By-law 65 shall be a first charge upon all the funds of the Association.

69. *The legal representatives or beneficiaries of a member who may die through accident or injury, and who may be entitled to a claim under by-law 65, shall have no claim under By-laws 66, 67 and 68, unless the benefit thereunder shall exceed the amount payable under By-law 65, in which event the payment of the "Mortuary Benefit" shall be in full satisfaction and discharge of all claims against the Association, inclusive of that under By-law 65 ; and in case the "mortuary benefit" is less in amount than the claim arising as aforesaid under By-law 65, payment under that By-law shall be in full satisfaction and discharge of all claims against the Association, including that under the said By-laws 66, 67 and 68.

70. *Should the mortality in any year exceed that estimated according to By-law 67, the remaining half of the annual surplus from the membership fees shall be used to pay the benefits fixed for that year ; and in the event of the same proving insufficient for that purpose, resort shall finally be had to the "Permanent Reserve Fund."

71. ** The balance of the "Annual Benefit Allotment" and the other half of the annual surplus from membership fees remaining at the end of any financial year, not used or required for any purposes of the Association, or to meet claims that may have arisen under any By-law during that year, shall be added to and form part of the "Permanent Reserve Fund."

ARTICLE XVI.—GENERAL PROVISIONS AS TO BONUSES AND BENEFITS.

72. ** Should a claim upon a death made under By-law 65 be disallowed by the Board as coming within the exceptions contained in that By-law, the claimant may have the same amended or another substituted therefor, so that such claim may be made under the provisions of By-law 6, it being the intention of these By-laws that the man-

ner or cause of death shall not in any way affect the validity of any claim that may be presented under By-law 66.

Provided al ys that the amount which may be paid upon such amended or substituted claim shall be taken in full satisfaction of all claims against the Association, and such amendment or substitution shall be made by the claimant within three months of the disallowance of the original claim.

73. *Claims under these By-laws are payable only at the offices of the Association at Toronto.

74. *In the event of any death, accident or injury occur ring, for which claims may be made under these By-laws, immediate notice thereof shall be given in writing, by the proper party, addressed to the Secretary at Toronto, stating the full name, occupation and address of the member. And unless direct and positive proof of the same, and of the death or duration of total disability, shall be furnished to this Association within six months from the happening thereof, all claims under these By-laws shall be and become, by reason of the default, waived and forfeited.

75. *No claim shall be payable under these By-laws unless a medical adviser of this Association shall be allowed to examine the person of the member, in respect of any alleged injury or cause of death, when and so often as may be reasonably required.

76. *All claims under these By-laws must be submitted to the Board of Directors, who shall have authority, and whose duty it will be to investigate the same, and decide upon their validity; and if the same are allowed, to order their payment. The powers of the said Board herein shall be those of arbitrators, and their decisions shall have the force and effect of an award.

77. *Claims under these By-laws shall be payable with- ixty days after satisfactory proof shall have been fur- d as aforesaid.

*The party entitled to receive any accident bonus or mortuary benefit shall previously furnish the Association with a legal discharge thereof.

ARTICLE XVII.—DEALING WITH OFFENDERS.

79. Any member who shall use abusive or improper anguage in the meetings of the Association, or who shall be guilty of disrespect towards the presiding officer, or of habitual drunkenness or immorality, or who shall abuse, or attempt to abuse, in any way the advantages or privileges of the Association, shall be liable to a charge, and, after due trial, may be fined, reprimanded, suspended or expelled, as the Association may determine.

80. Any member guilty of abusing, or attempting to abuse, the privileges of the Association, is liable to immediate suspension by the President, awaiting the action of the Board of Directors and the Association.

81. No member shall be put on trial unless a charge, or charges, duly specifying his alleged offence, or offences, shall be first submitted to the Association in writing, signed by one or more of its members.

82. Any charge, or charges, so preferred, shall be referred to a committee of five members to be appointed at the first general meeting, of whom three shall form a quorum, which committee shall, with as little delay as the case will admit, furnish accused with a copy of the charge, or charges, summon the parties, and examine and consider the matter in question.

83. If, after the reasonable notice of summons, the party accused fails to appear or to give satisfactory reply, the case may be gone on with in his absence.

84. The committee shall, after due investigation, submit a report of its proceedings, together with the evidence obtained, and a resolution, recommending what action, in their opinion, should be taken.

85. Should the decision of the Committee not involve suspension or expulsion of the accused member, and should no appeal be made therefrom, it shall be final without further action of the Association.

86. Should the committee be convinced of the necessity of suspending or expelling a member, a motion to that effect shall be submitted, signed by at least three of their number.

87. Any motion for the suspension or expulsion of a member, shall be announced at the regular meeting previous to that on which it comes up for decision, which last meeting the member under charges shall be summoned to attend, and at the time appointed, whether the implicated member be present or not, the Association may proceed to consider and determine the matter.

88. The Association shall have power to vary the penalty, to one more or less severe than that contained in the motion submitted by the Committee.

89. In all cases of the expulsion of members, the Secretary of the Association shall immediately notify all other Travellers' Associations thereof, as well as the Railway or other Companies interested.

ARTICLE XVIII.—ADDITIONAL ACCIDENT BONUSES.

90. The Board may, on behalf of the Association, enter int contracts with such Accident Insurance Companies as they may determine, to insure such of its members as may desire to avail themselves of the benefit of such contracts against accidents or casualties arising to such members whereby they may suffer loss, or injury, or be disabled, or die, upon and subject to the provisions of this By-law, viz :

(a) Such contracts shall, in any case, provide for the payment to such members, or their beneficiaries, or representatives, as the case may be—

1. Upon death, the sum of $5,000.
2. A weekly indemnity for temporary total disability of $25 per week (maximum period 26 weeks).
3. And for such other payments in the event of permanent or other injury, as may be agreed upon.

(b) The terms, conditions and agreements upon and subject to which such insurance shall be made and the said sums shall be payable, shall be settled and determined by the said Board with the said Companies, with such variations as may from time to time be agreed upon, all of which shall apply uniformly to the aforesaid members, who shall hold, and be entitled to receive such benefits upon and subject to the said terms, conditions and agreements in every respect.

(c) Any member desirous of obtaining the benefit of such Accident Insurance contracts may do so upon making application therefor to the Association, in writing, in such form as the Board may determine.

(d) The annual premium for such insurance shall not exceed $12, and shall be payable in equal quarterly instalments, in advance, on the 1st days of March', June, September and December in each year. The premium for the proportionate unexpired time of the quarter in which the application is made shall be payable with the application.

(c) In the matter of the said insurance the Association shall, for all purposes, be deemed to be acting therein as the agents for such members only, and not as insurers.

ARTICLE XIX.—ALTERATION OF BY-LAWS.

91. No motion to repeal, suspend, annul, amend or add to these Be-laws, or any part thereof, nor to alter the rules of order, shall be put to vote, except at the Annual Meeting of this Association. Two months' notice of the exact alterations shall be given to the Secretary, in writing, by the member proposing the same, and a printed circular containing the proposed changes shall be sent by the Secretary to every member of this Association, at least three week prior to the date of the General Annual Meeting, and such alterations of the By-laws may be accepted with or without amendment, upon at least two-thirds of the members present voting in favor thereof.

Note—The By-laws preceded by an asterisk * were included in the schedule to the amending act of 1883, ante-page 25 ; and all by-laws or sub-sections of by-laws prefixed * * were amended or added to by leave of the Governor-General in Council, under Sec. 10 of said act. None of such by-laws can be amended or repealed unless with the approval of the Governor-General in Council under said Sec. 10, or by Legislation.

SIXTEENTH ANNUAL REPORT

OF THE

BOARD OF DIRECTORS.

1888.

The Directors have much pleasure in calling the attention of the members to the fact that the close of the present financial year finds the Association in possession of a surplus of $152,729.63. Early in the history of the Association, it was determined to forego insurance until the funds amounted to $50,000. This point was reached in 1882. The report of 1885 marked a second period ; the surplus amounted to $100,000, and was a matter of much congratulation among the members ; upon attaining to the third $50,000, the present Directors are glad to be able to report continued improvement in the resources of the Association, despite the heavy mortality bills which have been met during the past two years.

The following is an abstract of the Receipts and Disbursements for the financial year ending November 30th, 1888.

RECEIPTS.

Ordinary Certificates	....	$26,680 00
Honorary	....	500 00
Duplicate "	....	52 00
		$27,232 00
Interest	....	7,016 52
		$34,248 52

DISBURSEMENTS.

Advertising	$	59	05
Commission		341	00
General Expense		754	91
Special Expense		1,725	48
Printing		520	18
Stationery		116	52
Papers		93	70
Rent		384	76
Salary		1,500	00
Accident Bonus		1,730	66
Mortuary Benefits		10,884	00
Balance		16,138	26

$34,248 52

It will be observed that the balance carried t₡ capital amounts to $16,138.26, being an increase over last year's balance of $513.71. The membership also shows an in-crease, the total now being 2,718.

Under the provisions of By-law 67, the Annual Benefit Allotment was ascertained as being $16,704.9₡ for 1888. and the maximum Mortuary Benefit fixed at $1,200.

The following shows the payments under the allotment :

Beneficiary of	H. Ritchie	$	960	00
"	A. R. Morrison		600	00
"	C. C. Davison		240	00
"	John Walker		1,200	00
"	E. R. Chillas		600	00
"	James Young		600	00
"	W. H. Jackman		720	00
"	E. Bendelari		1,080	00
"	C. Denison		560	00
"	D. L. Beemer		1,200	00
"	H.J. Knowles		360	00
"	Z. Hemphill		840	00
"	F. Wilson		84	00
"	R. H. Cozzens		960	00
"	R. Lalor		1,080	00

$10,884 00

The payments under the Accident Bonus By-law were as follows :

Beneficiary of J. W. Stewart .... $ 1,000 00
"   Minor Claims 730 66
                                   —————— $1,730 66

The total sum paid under the insurance by-laws, as above noted, amounts to $12,614.66. A reference to the abstract shows that the amount received for interest on investments was $7,016.52. These figures are placed in contrast for the purpose of giving prominence to the soundness of the policy hitherto pursued of steadily aiming at increasing the interest-earning power of the Association, thereby insuring stability to its insurance plans, augmenting the security of Certificate holders, and placing the permanent position of the Association itself beyond the possibility of danger.

The calls upon the Relief or Charitable Fund have been more frequent than last year, although the Directors have been able to grant assistance to every deserving case brought before them. It is very desirable that a fund sufficient to meet all emergencies should be on hand, and in order that every member should have an opportunity of contributing the small sum at which the subscriptions have been placed, an envelope and memo for signature is enclosed herewith. The Secretary will acknowledge the receipt of each remittance.

Our relations with the Transportation Companies are harmonious, the privileges being continued upon the basis of the settlement approved of by the adjourned annual meeting of May 12th.

The Maximum Mortuary Benefit for 1889 has been placed at $1,200.00. In arriving at this amount the Directors have, as heretofore, acted under the advice of Wm. McCabe, Esq., Managing Director of the North American Life Assurance Company, who continues to be a steadfast friend of the Association.

J. C. BLACK.   JAMES SARGANT,
    President.   *Secretary*.
Toronto, Dec. 15th, 1888.

FINANCIAL STATEMENT, 1888.

County of Perth Debentures
   (Estimated value)............$33,354 03
Freehold Loan Co. Debentures
   (with accrued interest) 15,312 50
Union Loan Co.............. 5,104 17
                               $53,770 70

(The above are deposited with
   the Dominion Government.)
Farmers' Loan Co. Debenture
   (with accrued interest)......$10,041 66
People's Loan Co............ 10,208 33
Western Canada Loan Co..... 15,312 50
Hamilton Provident Loan Co.. 20,416 66
Union Loan Co.... .... 10,166 67
Freehold Loan Co........... 15,062 50
Imperial Loan Co............ 10,208 33
                                $91,416 65
Dominion Bank (Deposit) 6,637 43

                                $151,824 78
Office Furniture 904 85

                                $152,729 63

        ROBERT H. GRAY,
                Treasurer.

RELIEF FUND STATEMENT, NOVEMBER 30, 1888.

NOVEMBER 30th, 1887.
   To Balance $341 55
   Subscriptions, 1888................. 265 00
                          $606 55
DISBURSEMENTS—
   Paid Relief Claims................ $300 00
   Postage 29 00
                          $329 00

   Balance $277 55

        JAMES SARGANT,
                Secretary.

AUDITORS' REPORT.

.Toronto, December 15, 1888.

To the President and Directors of the Commercial Travellers' Association of Canada :

Gentlemen :

We have the honor to report that every month we have carefully examined the books, accounts and vouchers of your Association for the year 1888, as kept by the Secretary, including those used for the Relief Benefit Fund, and found them correct.

We have compared the Balance sheet prepared by the Secretary with the Ledger balances, and find them to correspond.

We have inspected the Debentures deposited with the Dominion Bank for safe keeping, and found the amount to be ninety thousand dollars ($90,000), which with the accrued interest amounts to $91,416.65, as shown in statement.

We testify to the general carefulness manifested by the Secretary in keeping the Account Books, and to his earnest desire at all times to furnish the necessary facilities to aid us in the discharge of our duties.

.We have the honor to be, gentlemen,

Your obedient servants,

WM. ANDERSON, ⎱ Auditors.
JAS. E. DAY, ⎰

SEVENTEENTH ANNUAL REPORT

OF THE

BOARD OF DIRECTORS.
1889.

The Directors have much pleasure in submitting to the members the annual financial statements, and in again congratulating them upon the fact that the statements indicate continued prosperity and compare favorably with those of former years.

The surplus now amounts to $171,972.97, being a gain of $19,243 34. The membership roll shows an increase of 207, the total number now being 2,925.

The following is an abstract of the Receipts and Disbursements for the financial year ending November 30th, 1889 :

RECEIPTS.

Ordinary Certificates	$28,920	00
Honorary Certificates	520	00
Duplicate Certificates	66	00
	$29,506	00
Interest	7,975	75
	$37,481	75

DISBURSEMENTS.

Advertising	$ 113	50
Commission	388	50
General Expense	719	65
Special	1,511	39
Printing	284	65
Carried forward	3,017	69

Brought forward........	$ 3,017	69
Stationery..................	129	40
Papers.....................	140	20
Rent.......................	385	52
Secretary's Salary............	1,500	00
Assistant's "	110	00
Accident Bonuses.............	1,597	60
Mortuary Benefits.............	11,358	00
Balance.....................	19,243	34
	$37,481	75

Under the provision of By-law 67 the Annual Benefit Allotment was ascertained as being $17,884.82 for 1889, and the maximum Mortuary Benefit fixed at $1,200.00. The following shows the payments under the Allotment:

Beneficiary of H. C. Sheppard.....	$ 204	00
Robt. Raw....	1,200	00
A. Bernstein........	306	00
Jos. Purvis.........	960	00
Jos. Phillips......	1,200	00
G. T. Robinson.....	1,080	00
C. A. McElderry....	960	00
O. R. Peck...........	1,200	00
Thos. World........	1,200	00
L. K. Martin.......	360	00
Wm. T. McClary....	240	00
W.D. Peirce........	1,200	00
D. Howell..........	1,200	00
Chas. Davidson.......	48	00
	$11,358	00

The payments under the Accident Bonus By-law were as follows :

W. H. McIlroy.	$1,000	00
Minor Claims.	597	60
	$1,597	60

It is of course reasonable to expect that with the progress of time the payments under the Mortuary By-Laws should increase, the payments on this account, however,

have only been $474.00 greater than those of last year.
Under the Accident By-Laws, the payments have been
$133.06 less than those of the preceding year, the net in-
crease therefore of payments on Insurance Account being
only $340.94.

It will be observed that the amount earned as interest
on the invested funds of the Association is now becoming
an important feature of the Financial Statement. This
year it amounts to $7,975.75. Contrasting that sum with
the expenses of management, it becomes evident that the
Association is not only self-supporting, but that the receipts on Interest Account would not only have paid all
official expenses, but would have left a surplus of $2,692.-
94. Of course under the By-Laws, interest on investments is reserved for insurance purposes ; viewed from
that standpoint, the amount received on Interest Account
was sufficient to have paid two-thirds of the entire losses
of the year.

Accumulating a substantial Reserve Fund has been the
constant policy of the management of the Association.
The practical value of the Reserve Fund is becoming very
evident, the stability of the Association itself and the un-
questionable character of its Insurance Certificates are now
placed beyond the possibility of danger under any contin-
gency which prudence can foresee.

The increasing importance of the British Columbia
trade induced the Directors to despatch the Secretary to
Victoria for the purpose of reporting on the advisability
of opening an Agency in that city. Acting upon the report of that official, a Local Secretary and two Provisional
Directors were appointed pending the action of the Annual Meeting, to which a By-Law will be submitted
giving legal effect to the steps temporarily taken.

The applications for relief from indigent members and
their families have been more numerous than usual. The
Directors have been hampered in the assistance which
they were able to extend by the smallness of the fund for
charitable purposes at their disposal. They trust, however, that the Circular on this subject recently sent out
may evoke a generous response from the membership.

Our relations with the Transportation Companies are of the most friendly nature, the present arrangements having been renewed for the incoming year.

The maximum Mortuary Benefit for 1890 has been placed at $1,200. In deciding on this amount the Directors have been guided, as heretofore, by the actuarial advice of Mr. Wm. McCabe, Managing Director of the North American Life Assurance Company.

A. A. ALLAN,   JAMES SARGANT,
President.   *Secretary.*

TORONTO, Dec. 16th, 1889.

FINANCIAL STATEMENT, 1889.

ASSETS.

County of Perth Debentures
(estimated value............ $33,246 95
Freehold Loan Co. Debentures   15,312 50
Union Loan Co. Debentures ...   5,104 17

(The above are deposited with the Dominion Government.)

Imperial Loan Co. Debent.		10,208 33
Freehold Loan Co. Debent.		15,062 50
Union Loan Co. Debentures		10,166 67
Hamilton Pro. L. Co. Deb.	Deposited in the Dominion Bank. Toronto.	20,416 66
B'lding & Loan Assn. Deb.		15,250 00
W. Canada Loan Co. Deb.		15,312 50
People's Loan Co. Deb. ..		10,208 33
Farmers' Loan Co. Deb. ..		10,041 66
Imperial Loan Co. Deb. ..		10,166 67
Dominion Bank (Deposit)		551 18
		———— $171,048 12
Office Furniture		924 85
		————
		$171,972 97

ROBERT H. GRAY, *Treasurer.*

RELIEF FUND STATEMENT, NOVEMBER 30, 1889.

NOVEMBER 30TH, 1888.

To Balance	$277 55	
Subscriptions, 1889	227 00	
Interest	3 70	
		$508 25

DISBURSEMENTS—

Paid Relief Claims	$400 00	
Postage	24 50	
		$424 50
Balance		$83 75

JAMES SARGANT, *Secretary.*

AUDITORS' REPORT.

TORONTO, December 16th, 1889.

To the President and Directors of the Commercial Travellers' Association of Canada :

GENTLEMEN,

We have the honor to report that every month we have carefully examined the books, accounts and vouchers of your Association for the year 1889, as kept by the Secretary, including those used for the Relief Benefit Fund, and found them correct.

We have compared the Balance Sheet prepared by the Secretary with the Ledger Balances, and find them to correspond.

We have inspected the Debentures deposited with the Dominion Bank for safe keeping, and found the amount to be one hundred and fifteen thousand dollars ($115,000) which with the accrued interest amounts to $116,833.32, as shown in statement.

We testify to the general carefulness manifested by the Secretary in keeping the Account Books, and to his earnest desire at all times to furnish the necessary facilities to aid us in the discharge of our duties.

We have the honor to be, gentlemen, your obedient servants,

WM. ANDERSON, } AUDITORS.
JAS. E. DAY,

EIGHTEENTH ANNUAL REPORT

OF THE

BOARD OF DIRECTORS.
1890.

Your Board of Management take pleasure in reporting that progress crowns the work of the year 1890 in every department of the Association, as exhibited in the figures of the following statements, a careful examination of which your Directors earnestly ask on the part of each member.

The membership has gained 208, the roll now showing 3,133 members. A corresponding gain will also be found in receipts, interest, assets and surplus.

The surplus now amounts to $181,979.91, being a gain of $10,006.94.

The following is an abstract of the receipts and disbursements for the financial year ending November 30th, 1890 :

RECEIPTS.

Ordinary Certificates	$30,660 00	
Honorary "	870 00	
Duplicate "	64 00	
	31,594 00	
Interest....	8,780 37	
		$40,374 37

DISBURSEMENTS.

Advertising	42 00	
Commission.....................	432 00	
General Expenses....	887 81	
Special "	1,041 82	
Printing......................	389 00	
Stationery	89 08	
Papers....	163 20	
Rent.........................	612 02	
Carried forward		3,656 93

Brought forward	$ 3,656	93
Secretary's Salary	1,500	00
Assistant's "	282	00
Accident Bonuses ....'........	2,980	50
Mortuary Benet `..............	21,948	00
Balance .... :..	10,006	94
	—$40,378	37

Under the provision of By-law 67, the Annual Benefit Allotment was ascertained as being $20,087.34 for 1889, and the Maximum Mortuary Benefit fixed at $1,200.00.

The following shows the payments under the Allotment, being $1,860.66 more than the entire Allotment, and which has been paid, under By-law No. 70, from out of the balance of the year's receipts.

C. G. Cobban	$,200	00
Mark Marks	1,200	00
J. P. Wheaton	600	00
J. A. Mackie	720	00
John Young	1,200	00
C. Tetu	1,200	00
W. McDonald	600	00
T. Mitchell.... .. ,.	1,200	00
E. J. Potts	1,200	00
W. L. Cusack	1,200	00
W. F. H. Harper	204	00
Isaac Abbott	1,200	00
J. Pollie	600	00
J. E. Reynolds	1,080	00
W. B. Palmer	1,200	00
C. Gull	720	00
A. Skinner	240	00
J. Campbell	1,200	00
W. Carscaden	960	00
W. E. Buchan	600	00
W. J. Campbell	1,080	00
S. A. Potter	600	00
J. S. Norrie	144	00
J. Pointer	1,200	00
P. Slattery	600	00
	—$21,948	00

The payments under the Accident Bonus By-law were as follows :

G. B. Island..................$1,000 00
J. W. Murray.............. .. 1,000 00
Minor Claims 980 50
                                ————$ 2,980 50

The following Table will show the amounts paid out for Accident and Mortuary Benefit claims since the Association became its own insurer, in the year 1879.

Years.	Death Accident.	Death Mortuary.	Mortuary Payments.	Accident Payments.	Minor Accident Payments.	TOTAL.
1879	1		....	1,000.00	517.13	1,517.13
80	2		....	2,000.00	400.70	2,400.70
81	1	3	1,400.00	1,000.00	426.06	2,826.06
82	2	2	1,400.00	2,000.00	133.53	2,533.53
83	2	7	3,000.00	2,000.00	1,005.93	6,005 93
84	1	11	6,800.00	1,000.00	558.00	8,358.00
85	....	10	8,350.00	....	913.83	9,263.83
86	1	7	4,840.00	1,000.00	889.63	6,726.63
87	......	17	11,484.00	....	700.50	12,184.50
88	1	15	10,884.00	1,000.00	730.66	12,614.66
89	1	14	11,358.00	1,000 00	597.60	12,955.60
90	2	25	21,948.00	2,000.00	980.50	24,928.50

As foreshadowed in previous reports, it was reasonable to expect that with the progress of time the payments under the Mortuary Benefit By-law would increase, a glance at the Table will show the expectation has been realized, but it is only fair to add that the experience of the Association in its insurance branches during the past year has been shared by all regular Life Insurance Companies, who also report extraordinary increased death· losses, but it is gratifying to know that while our payments grow larger year by year, the Reserve Fund of the Association also increases, as the following Table will exhibit :

YEAR.	MEMBERSHIP.	SURPLUS.
1873	588	959.96
1874	432	3,700.00
1875	872	5,774.61
1876	630	7,949.96
1877	873	11,013.69
1878	1,104	13,540.51
1879	1,226	22,555.60
1880	1,419	32,572.61
1881	1,740	49,239.10
1882	2,041	61,783.30
1883	2,114	73,187.53
1884	2,202	86,698.70
1885	2,289	100,510.00
1886	2,516	119,368.97
1887	2,715	135,591.37
1888	2,718	152,729.63
1889	2,925	171,972.97
1890	3,133	181,979.91

All this has been accomplished under the conservative policy marked out in each succeeding year by the Officers and Directors, and steadily adhered to by the members, so that with the Cash Permanent Reserve Fund of $176,-813.17, each member can place every confidence in the value of his Mortuary Benefit Certificate.

At the annual meeting held on December 29th, 1889, a resolution was adopted, looking to the formation of an Annuity Scheme, and requesting your Directors to lay the matter before the Association's Actuary. The resolution was complied with by your Board. Mr. McCabe, after a careful consideration, tendered his opinion in the following letter :

James Sargant Esq.

Secretary Commercial Travellers' Association, Toronto.

DEAR SIR,—I have your esteemed favor, enclosing a resolution of the Board on the subject of annuities, upon which my opinion is requested. In reply I respectfully refer the Board to the memorandum sent them on the

14th of December last, and in view of the facts therein stated, I think it inexpedient to add any new feature, especially in view of the heavy mortality of the current year. In my opinion it is of the utmost importance to keep matters as they are as near as possible until cur invested funds shall have amounted to a quarter of a million dollars.

Yours truly,

WM. McCABE, *Actuary.*

Applications from indigent members and their families continue to be made on the Relief fund. We urgently suggest a generous response by all the members, so that your Board (who act as Trustees) may have sufficient funds to meet all calls ; they trust that the circular recently sent out will meet with a very hearty response.

The present arrangements existing between the Transportation Companies and the Association have been renewed for the ensuing year ; our relations continue of the most friendly nature.

For some time past it has been felt that the rooms we now occupy are entirely inadequate to the growing requirements of the Association, and at the annual meeting two years ago it was strongly urged upon your Board that more suitable premises should be secured.

With this in view a committee was appointed and a number of favorable places were examined, but the difficulty of securing a central location at a reasonable cost made the selection a trying one to make.

After a most thorough and careful investigation, the premises formerly occupied by the Central Bank, 51 Yonge Street were selected, and have been fitted up in such a manner as will provide all the accommodation we require, in one of the very best locations in the city, at a comparatively small addition to our present expenses.

As a large number of our members think it desirable that the Association should purchase a permanent home, your Board have secured the refusal of these premises at a price that appears to them favorable, particulars of which will be laid before you.

The maximum Mortuary Benefit for 1891 has been placed at $1,200.00. In deciding on this amount the Directors have been guided, as heretofore, by the actuarial advice of Mr. Wm. McCabe, Managing Director of the North American Life Assurance Company.

There are but few things necessary to assure our future success, the continued zeal and loyalty of all our members, cautious and prudent legislation and a rigid observance of the laws by which we are governed.

A. A. ALLAN,   JAMES SARGANT,
President.   *Secretary.*
TORONTO, Dec. 16th, 1890.

FINANCIAL STATEMENT, 1890.

ASSETS—

County of Perth Debentures (estimated value)	$33,135	27
Freehold Loan Co. Debentures	15,312	50
Union " "	5,104	17
(The above are deposited with the Dominion Government).		
Imperial Loan Co. Debentures	10,208	33
Freehold " "	15,062	50
Union " "	10,166	67
Hamilton Provident Loan Co. Debentures	20,416	66
Building & Loan Assn. Debentures	15,250	00
Western Canada Loan Co. Debentures	15,312	50
Peoples' Loan Co. Debentures	10,208	33
Farmers' Loan Co. Debentures	10,041	66
Imperial Loan Co. Debentures	10,166	67
Land Security Loan Co. Debentures	10,041	66
British Canadian Loan Co. Debentures	5,104	16
	$185,531	08

The above are Deposited in the Dominion Bank.

OTHER ASSETS—
Office Fur iiture..............$ 1,029 10
Building Ii ip. Account........ 4,137 62   5,166 72
          ————— $190,697 80.

LIABILITIES—
Dominion Bank............... ....$ 8,717 89
                 $181,979 91

RELIEF FUND STATEMENT, NOVEMBER 30TH, 1890.

RECEIPTS—
Nover 'ber 30th, 1889.
To Balance..........................$ 83 75
Subscriptions, 1890..... .. .. 532 00
Interest............................ 7 04
           ————— $622 79

DISBURSEMENTS—
Paid Relief Claims.............. ..... $254 00

Balance........................... $368 79

JAMES SARGANT, *Secretary.*

AUDITORS' REPORT

TORONTO, December 16th, 1890.

*To the President and Directors of the Commercial Travellers'
Association of Canada :*

GENTLEMEN,—

We hereby certify that the books, accounts and vouchers of the Association have been regularly audited month
by month during the year 1890, and found correct. We
have compared the Secretary's Annual Financial Statement with his books of account, and his Cash Book, with
the Bank Pass Book, and found them respectively to
agree. The books of the Relief Fund have likewise been
regularly audited and found correct. We have this day

C

examined the debentures held by the Association, and now deposited for safe keeping in the Dominion Bank, and found the amount ($131,979.14) to agree with the books, say One Hundred and Thirty Thousand Dollars and accrued interest. We testify to the general carefulness manifested by the Secretary in keeping the account books and to his earnest desire at all times to furnish the necessary facilities to aid us in the discharge of our duties.

We have the honor to be, gentlemen, your obedient servants,

WM. ANDERSON,
WM. BADENACH. } AUDITORS.

NINETEENTH ANNUAL REPORT

OF THE

BOARD OF DIRECTORS.

1891,

The Board of Directors have great pleasure in placing before the members this the Nineteenth Annual Report—feeling assured that a careful perusal of it will be to them a matter of great satisfaction.

The present year is marked, like its predecessors, with substantial progress, and while the demands upon our Funds have been larger than usual, we still show a steadily increasing surplus, as also a gratifying addition to our membership. We have to-day enrolled as members 3,290, showing an increase during the year of 157.

The Receipts and Disbursements for the current financial year, ending 30th Nov., are as follows :—

RECEIPTS.

Ordinary Certificates	$31,850 00	
Honorary "	1,050 00	
Duplicates "	74 00	
		$32,974 00
Interest		7,201 62
		$40,175 62

DISBURSEMENTS—

Commission	$ 437 50	
Special Expense	1,951 63	
Printing	379 75	
Stationery	109 73	
Papers	123 10	
Rent	691 90	
Secretary's Salary	1,775 00	
Assistant's "	334 00	
General Expense	916 71	
Advertising	54 30	
Mortuary Benefits	21,648 00	
Accident	1,777 30	
Balance	9,976 70	
		$40,175 62

The purchase and reorganization of our recently acquired premises have absorbed a portion of our accumulated funds.

By-Law 67 provides for the Annual Mortuary Benefit Allotment, which was ascertained as being $21,858.40, and the Maximum Benefit placed at $1200 for the year 1891.

Payments during the year under the Allotment have been as follows :—

J. W. Thomson	$1,200 00	
P. B. Clark	1,200 00	
J. Van Staden	1,200 00	
W. Lundy	1,200 00	
C. E. Stevens	840 00	
B. Bailley	1,200 00	
John Besford	1,200 00	
Carried forward		$ 8,040 00

Brought forward	$8,040 00
J. M. Hudson	240 00
F. Lazarus	48 00
W. W. Widgerey	1,200 00
D. McInnes	360 00
John James	840 00
J. H. Forbes	840 00
T. G. Ralston	840 00
J. J. Upfield	600 00
P. Kemp	1,200 00
W. J. Scarfe	1,200 00
T. Mealey	1,200 00
W. H. Hambly	1,080 00
G. E. Gillespie	1,200 00
E. Martin	840 00
R. Duncan	360 00
R. L. VanCott	480 00
J. Korman	1,080 00
	——$21,648 00

As the age of membership increases from year to year, and as our Mortuary Benefit scheme presents such an admirable and absolutely safe system of Insurance, it is but reasonable to suppose that the amount of disbursements to Beneficiaries will continue to grow larger. However, we are pleased to state that each succeeding year we are able to report a marked addition to our Reserve Fund, and feel assured the future income of the Association from different sources may always be expected to largely exceed the outgoings. A glance at the exhibit will show the additions to our membership and surplus.

With the fact before us of large payments from year to year, which we cannot but suppose will gradually increase, your Directors, guided by the excellent advice of Mr. Wm. McCabe, Fellow of the Institute of Actuaries of Great Britain, Managing Director of the North American Life Assurance Co., have placed the Maximum Mortuary Benefit for the year 1892 at $1,200.00.

The following amounts have been paid under the provisions of the Accident Bonus By-Law :—

ACCIDENT CLAIMS.

·A. E. Bunker	$1,000 00
Minor Claims	777 30

$1,777 30

Your Directors, anxiously desiring to provide cheap and absolutely safe additional Accident Insurance for the membership at large, have succeeded in completing a most favorable arrangement with the London Guarantee and Accident Co. The amount of the Policy is for $5,000, and covers every desirable detail in modern Accident Insurance, and, while the rate is cheapest in Canada, the security is beyond peradventure. Circulars with details of the scheme are already in your hands, and it is earnestly hoped that every member of the Association will avail himself of this additional Accident Insurance.

And we have also to report the completion of improvements and occupation of our present building. Outside of the required space for our own Offices, Reading Room, etc., all the rest of the premises are satisfactorily leased for a term of years. The Board feel assured that the members cannot but be pleased with the new, comfortable and spacious quarters provided for them, in response to a demand for such for some years past.

A very important matter has been receiving the attention of your Board for some months, looking to a very substantial addition to our membership and income, namely :—the amalgamation with us of the North-Western Traveller's Association of Winnipeg. A deputation from your Board visited Winnipeg in July, and in consultation with the officers of the N. W. Association, the whole scheme of amalgamation was thoroughly discussed. The matter is still under consideration, and we confidently look forward to a satisfactory basis of agreement and their early amalgamation with us.

Your Board have pleasure in reporting a continuance of the pleasant relations existing between our Association and all Transportation companies, as also a renewal of all the privileges for the coming year. With vigilant regard to the best interests of the Association, and if possible to

secure still further concessions from the said companies,
a deputation from the Board, supplemented by representatives from sister Associations, visited Montreal early this
month, and had a conference with the officials of the
various railways in regard to railway fares, excess baggage, Friday to Monday tickets, etc., with a view of securing, if possible, better terms.

Your Board have great pleasure in stating that the rate
of Interest on our Investments, all of which are of the
most approved character, is still maintained.

We desire to record here with special pride that not a
single certificate has been cancelled for breach of railway
privileges during the year.

We desire to call special attention to the Relief Fund.
It is not our intention to discuss here the need of such a
fund. We, however, beg to emphasize the fact that a
large amount of real good has been accomplished by it,
and trust that every member of the Association will become a regular subscriber to this worthy object, the Annual Fee of which is only one dollar.

We append a statement of this fund for the year 1891.

We cannot too strongly urge the most devoted loyalty
and zeal amongst all the members to the best interests,
rules and laws of the Association, and with the continued
careful and painstaking attention from your officers and
members alike, we see for the future of the C. T. Association of Canada the most gratifying results and abound-
ing prosperity.

JOHN BURNS,
    President.
             JAS. SARGANT,
                Secretary.

FINANCIAL STATEMENT, 1891.

ASSETS—

County of Perth Debentures (es-
timated value) .... $ 33,018 79
Freehold Loan Co.   " 15,312 50
Union   "   "   " 5,104 17
(The above are deposited with the
Dominion Government).

        Carried forward........ ————— $53,435 46

Brought forward........$53,435 46
Union Loan Co. Debentures..... 10,166 67
Hamilton Provident " 20,416 66
Bldg. & Loan Assn. Debentures.. 15,250 00
People's " " " .. 10,208 33
Farmers' " " " .. 10,041 66
Imperial " " " .. 10,166 67
Land Security................ 10,041 66
British Canadian.............. 5,104 16
(The above are deposited with the
  Dominion Bank).
Real Estate................... 49,588 46
                                        ————$194,419 73
OTHER ASSETS—
Office Furniture...............$ 2,185 95
Inventors' Assoc.......... .... 60 00   2,245 95

                                        ————$196,665 68
LIABILITIES—
Dominion Bank........................ 4,709 07

                                        $191,956 61

RELIEF FUND STATEMENT, NOVEMBER 30th, 1891.

1890—November 30th,
To Balance..........................$368 79
1891—Subscriptions.................. 377 00
  Interest.......................... 15 30
                                        ——— $761 09
Paid Relief Claims..... .... 500 00

Balance.............................. $261 09
                        JAS. SARGANT, *Secretary.*

AUDITORS' REPORT.

TORONTO, December 11th, 1891.
To the President and Directors of the Commercial Travellers'
  Association of Canada.
GENTLEMEN,—
  We hereby certify that the books, accounts and vouchers
of the Association have been regularly audited month by

month during the year 1891, and found correct. We have compared the Secretary's Annual Financial Statement with his books of account, and his Cash Book, with the Bank Pass Book, and found them respectively to agree. The books of the Relief Fund have likewise been regularly audited, and found correct. We have this day examined the debentures held by the Association, and now deposited for safe keeping in the Dominion Bank, and found the amount ($91,395.81) to agree with the books, say Ninety Thousand Dollars and accrued interest. We testify to the general carefulness manifested by the Secretary in keeping the account books and to his earnest desire at all times to furnish the necessary facilities to aid us in the discharge of our duties.

We have the honor to be, gentlemen, your obedient servants,

WM. ANDERSON, }
WM. BADENACH, } AUDITORS.

TWENTIETH ANNUAL REPORT

OF THE

BOARD OF DIRECTORS.

1892.

The Report that your Directors have now the pleasure of submitting for your consideration, is to them an unusually gratifying one, and they feel assured that a careful perusal of it by the entire membership will meet with their marked approval.

It will be a source of great satisfaction to every member to note the large surplus that is carried this year to the Permanent Reserve Fund, an amount largely in excess of either of the past two years, amounting to $14,695.62

while our membership keeps on increasing, the roll showing 3,402 members, a total increase during the year of 112.
The Receipts and Disbursements for the current financial year, ending 30th November. 1892 are as follows :—

RECEIPTS.

Ordinary Certificates	32 35 00		
Honorary "	1,290 00		
Duplicate "	66 00		
		$34,091 00	
Freehold Loan Co. Debentures (matured)	15,000 00		
Union " " "	5,000 00		
Interest	7,003 84		
Rentals	3,620 00		
Additional Accident Insurance	1,481 00		
		$66,195 84	

DISBURSEMENTS.

Commission	$ 421 00	
Special Expense	1,.30 00	
Printing	361 70	
Stationery	161 58	
Papers and Periodicals	111 15	
Building Improvement Account	157 45	
Secretary's Salary	1,800 00	
Assistant's "	364 00	
Office Furniture	251 71	
General Expense	915 93	
Advertising	37 80	
Rental Expense (Water, Light-ing, Heating, Wages, &c.)	1,591 40	
Rent	1,500 00	
Central Canada Loan and Sav-ings Co. Debenture	20,000 00	
Mortuary Benefits	20,568 00	
Accident Bonus	1,998 50	
Balance	14,695 62	
		$66,195 84

By-law 67 provides for the Annual Mortuary Benefit
Allotment, which was ascertained as being $20,301.81,

and the maximum Benefit placed at $1,200 for the year
1892.

Payments during the year under the Allotment have
been as follows :—

F. Miller......................	$ 600 00
J. W. Stanley............. ...	720 00
D. Rome....	1,200 00
C. L. Thomas................	1,200 00
B. Boyd	840 00
W. Kennedy...................	720 00
H. W. Judd..................	1,200 00
John Evans, jr................	1,200 00
J. Zingsheim.................	1,200 00
W. R. Howell...........	1,200 00
H. Melton....................	66 00
Geo. S. Findlay..............	1,200 00
A. J. Neill....	840 00
J. Millett........	1,200 00
J. Beckley.............. ..	1,200 00
A. A. Miller................	1,200 00
J. S. Crawford..............	1,080 00
J. B. Mather.................	1,200 00
J. W. Bedson....	1,200 00
C. P. Whyte.................	1,200 00
W. E. Zimmerman	102 00
	————— $20,568 00

The attention of our members to the foregoing amounts,
paid to friends of deceased members, affords an ample il-
lustration of the real benefits we enjoy from our Mortuary
Allotment. Your Board have placed the Maximum Mortuary Benefit, for the year 1893, at $1,200.00 under the
advice of our Actuary, Mr. Wm. McCabe, F. I. A. of
Great Britain, Managing Director of the North American
Life Assurance Co.

Your Board desire to record with very sincere regret
the loss by death of two members of the Board, Mr. J.
B. Mather, Vice-President for Winnipeg, and Mr J. R.
Armstrong, Director for Guelph.

The following amounts have been paid under the provisions of the Accident Bonus By Law :—

ACCIDENT CLAIMS.

J. A. Wing............	$1,000 00
Minor Claims..................	998 50
	$1,998 50

Your Board have pleasure in stating that the amicable arrangements which have existed from year to year, with the Transportation Companies, are still maintained, and that all the privileges accorded the Association heretofore have been renewed, with the additional concession of a Friday to Monday one fare return ticket. Your Directors desire to place on record their sincere regrets for the loss of so able an administrator of Railway Passenger traffic as Mr. Wm. Edgar, late General Passenger Agent of the Grand Trunk Railway.

During the past year a large number of our members have taken advantage of the excellent arrangements made for Additional Accident Insurance, with great advantage to themselves, as also adding to the funds of the Association. Your Directors confidently look for a very large increase in this Department during the coming year. Every member placing his Accident Insurance with this Association is helping to build r the funds in which we are all so deeply interested.

Your Board have special pride in reporting that not a single certificate has been cancelled during the year, for abuse of privileges, and they desire to *strongly* impress upon every member the urgency for continued loyalty and zeal to all the interests and obligations of our Association.

Your Board desire to thank the members who have so kindly contributed in the past to the Relief Fund, and would respectfully urge that every member forward the small contribution of $1.00 for 1893.

JOHN BURNS,   JAS. SARGANT,

President.   *Secretary.*

FINANCIAL STATEMENT, 1892.

ASSETS :—

County of Perth Debentures (es-
timated value)................$32,897 21
Land Security Debentures...... 10,041 66
Imperial Loan   " 10,166 67
————————$ 53,105 54

(The above are deposited with the
Dominion Government.)

Hamilton Provident Loan De-
benture $20,416 66
People's   "   "   10,208 33
Farmers'   "   "   10,041 66
Union   "   "   10,166 67
Building and Loan   "   15,250 00
British Canadian   "   5,104 16
Canada Central "   "   20,416 67
Dominion Bank deposit........ 10,108 13

(The above are deposited with the
Dominiom Bank.)   ————————$101,712 28
Real Estate................   49,745 91

$204,563 73

OTHER ASSETS :—

Office Furniture..............   2,437 66
Inventors' Association........   60 00   2,497 66

$207,061 39

RELIEF FUND STATEMENT, NOVEMBER 30th, 1892.

November 30th, 1891,
To Balance...................$261 09
1892, Subscriptions................ 389 00
Interest.................... 17 53
————————$667 62
Paid Relief Claims............   255 00

Balance.................... $412 62

JAS. SARGANT, *Secretary.*

AUDITORS' REPORT.

TORONTO, December 13th, 1892.

To the President and Directors of the Commercial Travellers' Association of Canada.

GENTLEMEN,—

We hereby certify that the books, accounts and vouchers of your Association have been regularly audited every month during the year 1892, and found correct. We have compared the Secretary's Annual Financial Statement with his books of account, and his Cash Book with the Bank Pass Book, and found them respectively to agree. The Books of the Relief Fund, as well as those of the Additional Accident Insurance, have also been regularly audited and found correct. We have to-day examined the debentures held by the Association, and now deposited for safe keeping in the Dominion Bank, and found the amount, $91,604.15, to agree with the books, which, together with $53,105.54, deposited with the Dominion Government, make $154,817.82, including accrued interest, to the 30th of November last. We testify to the general carefulness displayed by the Secretary in keeping the account books, and to his earnest desire at all times to furnish the necessary facilities to aid us in the discharge of our duties.

We have the honor to be, gentlemen, your obedient servants,

WM. ANDERSON, }
WM. BADENACH, } AUDITORS.

OF THE

BOARD OF DIRECTORS.

1893.

The Board of Directors have much pleasure in submitting for the consideration of the members the Twenty-First Annual Report, and to congratulate them upon the favorable position of the Association on the attainment of its majority. The conservative policy hitherto followed has been amply justified, the increasing amounts annually payable as mortuary benefits are being promptly provided for, and a satisfactory balance carried each year to the permanent reserve fund. The present year has been one of the most successful in the history of the Association, the addition to capital being $16,118.53, while the membership roll shows an increase of 196, the total number being 3,598.

By-Law 67 provides for the Annual Mortuary Benefit Allotment, which was ascertained as being $20,568.26, and the maximum Benefit placed at $1,200.00 for the year 1893.

Payments during the year under the Allotment have been as follows :

P. Duncan	$1,200	00
J. H. Hughes	1,200	00
W. E. Turner	600	00
W. Monkhouse	252	00
J. Irwin	1,200	00
S. Leonard	1,200	00
Carried forward	$ 5,652	00

Brought forward..........$5,652 00

J. B. Armstrong	1,200 00
J. Stanbury	1,200 00
T. Worswick	1,200 00
W. McAulay	1,200 00
J. A. Casey	510 00
P. Bajus	1,200 00
C. T. Marshall	1,200 00
J. Mitchell	960 00
G. Dempster	1,200 00
E. D. Turner	1,080 00
L. W. Simonds	1,200 00
J. A. Sully	720 00
J. McDonnell	84 00
D. Munshaw	1,200 00
A. Bryce	204 00

$20,010 00

The following amounts have been paid under the provisions of the Accident Bonus By-Law :—

ACCIDENT CLAIMS :

H. Palmer	$1,000 00
G. M. Bligh	1,000 00
Minor Claims	1,647 50

$3,647 50

The amount paid in respect of Accident Bonuses is somewhat greater than usual, and the Directors trust that the importance of the additional Accident Insurance feature of the Association's work will thereby be emphasized, and induce every member to take advantage of its provisions. The premium of $12.00 per annum securing $5,000 in the event of accidental death, or $25.00 weekly indemnity for accidental injury, is very much less than the regular rate, and is a special concession secured by the Association for the benefit of its members.

At the suggestion of friends of the Association in the eastern provinces, agencies have been opened at Quebec, St. John and Halifax, and we hope by this means to become more identified with the trade of Eastern Canada.

Doubtless, through oversight on the part of the members, the remittances to the Relief Fund for 1894 show a very considerable decrease up to the present time. The Directors feel that they have only to call attention to the subject, and that every member will send the small sum requested—one dollar—to be applied to the purposes of this Fund.

The Maximum Mortuary Benefit for 1894 has been continued at $1,200.00. In ascertaining this amount, the Directors have acted under the advice of Wm. McCabe, Esq., F.I.A., of Great Britain, Managing Director of the North American Life Assurance Co.

The transportation concessions granted by the Railway and Steamboat lines are of great importance to the commercial interests of the country, and the Directors cannot too strongly urge a continued faithful adherence to the terms of the agreement on the part of our members.

C. C. VAN NORMAN.   JAMES SARGANT,
            President.   *Secretary.*

TORONTO, Dec. 20th, 1893.

FINANCIAL STATEMENT, 1893.

PROFIT AND LOSS.

DR.

General Expenses	$ 2,358	57
Office "	3,395	28
Mortuary Benefits	20,010	00
Accident Bonuses	3,647	51
Rent	1,500	00
Office Furniture written off	454	91
Real Estate written off	385	42
Suspense	135	00
Balance to Permanent Reserve Fund	16,118	53
	$48,005	22

CR.

Certificates	$36,040	50
Interest	6,841	97
" Accrued	946	27
Rentals (net)	1,869	48
Additional Accident Insurance	2,307	00
	$48,005	22

BALANCE SHEET.

DR.

Permanent Reserve Fund	$223,179	92
Suspense	135	00
	$223,314	92

CR.

County of Perth Debentures	$32,770	53
Land Security Co. "	10,041	66
Imperial Loan Co. "	10,166	67
People's Loan Co. "	10,208	33
Farmers' Loan Co. "	10,041	66
British Canadian Co. "	15,291	66
Building & Loan As'n. "	15,250	00
Carried Forward	$103,770	51

Brought Forward.................	$103,770 51
Central Can. Loan Co. Debentures........	20,416 67
Toronto Saving Co. "	20,525 00
Landed Banking Co. "	10,027 12
First Mortgage Real Estate..............	16,333 33
Real Estate	50,000 00
Dominion Bank........................	107 29
Office Furniture.......................	2,000 00
Inventors' Association..................	60 00
H. M. Blight Estate...................	75 00

$223,314 92

RELIEF FUND STATEMENT, NOVEMBER 30th, 1893.

RECEIPTS.

November 30th, 1892—To Balance............$412 62
Subscriptions, 1893 .... 311 00
Interest 14 87

$738 49

DISBURSEMENTS.

Paid Relief Claims....................... $400 00
Balance 338 49

$738 49

J. C. BLACK,   JAMES SARGANT,
      Treasurer.   *Secretary.*
TORONTO, Nov. 30th, 1893.

AUDITORS' REPORT.

To the President and Directors of the Commercial Travellers' Association of Canada :

GENTLEMEN,—

We hereby certify that the books, accounts and vouchers of your Association have been regularly audited every month during the year 1893, and found correct. We

have compared the Secretary's Annual Financial Statement with his books of account, and his cash book with
the bank pass book, and found them respectively to agree.
The books of the Relief Fund, as well as those of the
Additional Accident Insurance, have also been regularly
audited and found correct. We have to-day received
certificate from the Dominion Bank certifying that they
hold for the Association securities to the amount of
$116,000, accrued interest thereon being $2,093.77, which
agrees with the books, together with $52,978.86 deposited
with the Dominion Government ; Real Estate, $50,000,
Furniture $2,000, Accounts $135 and Bank Balance
$107.29, make your total of assets $223,314.92. We testify
to the general carefulness displayed by the Secretary in
keeping the account books, and to his earnest desire at
all times to furnish the necessary facilities to aid us in
the discharge of our duties.

We have the honor to be, gentlemen, your obedient
servants,

WM. BADENACH, } AUDITORS.
WM. ANDERSON, }